T0274553

CALLING TO GOOD

CALLING TO GOOD

Islamic Mentoring and Guidance in a Modern World

M. FETHULLAH GÜLEN

Let there arise out of you a band of people inviting to all that is good,
enjoining what is right, and forbidding what is wrong:
They are the ones to attain felicity.

Al 'Imran 3:104

26 25 24 23 1 2 3 4

Published by Tughra Books
335 Clifton Ave.
Clifton, NJ, 07011, USA
www.tughrabooks.com

ISBN
Hardcover: 978-1-59784-958-6
Paperback: 978-1-59784-960-9
Ebook: 978-1-59784-994-4

Translated and edited by
Ayşe Özlem, Muhammed Çetin, Cemal Özgür, Justin Pahl

Library of Congress Cataloging-in-Publication Data

Names: Gülen, Fethullah, author.
Title: Calling to good : Islamic mentoring and guidance in a modern world / M. Fethullah Gülen.
Description: Clifton : Tughra Books, 2023. | Includes bibliographical references and index.
Identifiers: LCCN 2023037956 (print) | LCCN 2023037957 (ebook) | ISBN 9781597849586 (hardcover) | ISBN 9781597849944 (ebook)
Subjects: LCSH: Leadership--Religious aspects--Islam. | Mentoring--Religious aspects--Islam.
Classification: LCC BP190.5.L4 G85 2023 (print) | LCC BP190.5.L4 (ebook) | DDC 297.6/1--dc23/eng/20230914
LC record available at https://lccn.loc.gov/2023037956
LC ebook record available at https://lccn.loc.gov/2023037957

Contents

Preface 9

Chapter 1

Understanding the Call

1.1. The purpose of our existence 13
1.2. The need for conveying the message and benefits 21
1.3. The most valuable gift 30
1.4. Continuity 33
1.5. Moral obligation 40
1.6. Spiritual guidance, the individual, and society 45
1.7. Faith and hypocrisy 55
1.8. Stories of heavenly destructions 63
1.9. A measure of preserving religion 73

Chapter 2

Guidelines

2.1. Knowledge 79
2.2. Awareness of the era 86
2.3. The relationship between the Qur'an and the heart 88
2.4. Legitimate means for legitimate ends 90
2.5. Compensation 91
2.6. Knowing the person and empathy 97
2.7. The inter-play of faith, spiritual mentoring, and action 113
2.9. Relationship with authorities and the elite 136
2.10. Being resolute 138
2.11. Being insightful & conforming with innate human nature 140

Chapter 3

The Spiritual Characteristics of a Mentor

3.1. Compassion 149
3.2. Selflessness 153

3.3. Prayer 155
3.4. Being rational and realistic 156
3.5. Tolerance 157
3.6. Being caring 158
3.7. Spirituality 159
3.8. Enthusiasm 162
3.9. Purity of heart and spirit 164

Conclusion 167

Notes 173

Index 179

Preface

We are social beings and programmed to live interdependently with other humans. This compels us to contemplate on the societal dimension of the duty of spiritual mentoring and guidance in this worldly life, which is but an abode of trials. Our human nature wavers from one extremity to another and our feelings, desires, and ambitions recognize no limits. This human condition consequentially demands certain rules to keep these extremities in check. All the political, economic, moral, and legal concepts and doctrines designed to establish rule of law, social justice, and a virtuous society have been proposed throughout history for no other reason but to respond to this demand. Divine religions, on the other hand, have been largely ignored in the last few centuries although what they offer in this matter is arguably more comprehensive and conclusive than other doctrines.

Human beings can be anything, for better or worse. With our weaknesses, we can sink lower than the lowest; with our virtues, we can soar higher than the highest. Any approach to ethical nurturing that does not take these weaknesses and virtues into consideration is deficient.

Islam deals with the human, with the entire being. While—directly or indirectly—discouraging individuals from weaknesses, it encourages them to excel in virtues. The themes of hope and fear, Paradise and Hell, and mercy and wrath, come in a perfect balance in the Qur'an and traditions of Prophet Muhammad ﷺ, peace be upon him. The human who is consumed and paralyzed by fear and who is spoiled and made to be haughty by mere hope and empty expectations is not the type of human Islam aims for.

An ideal religious life can be maintained when observed in discipline. Reinforcing our spiritual lives and reaching metaphysical consciousness are possible if we can maintain our direction by observing certain guidelines. Rules and regulations may appear unpleasant at first sight; however, considering the benefits that will eventually come, it is obvious that these boundaries are in our favor just as prescriptions of encouragement are—they have a hidden beauty under their unpleasant face.

Failing to recognize the human with their multidimensional nature deprives us of realities about them and eventually from living a harmonious life. Islamic prescriptions, therefore, should be considered from the viewpoint of divinely inspired values based on the Qur'anic ethics and highest virtues as embodied in the example of Prophet Muhammad ﷺ. It is a duty upon us to show people the direction to that level of virtue and good character. What else is it if a virtuous life is not the purpose of being human?

The human being is a complex creature having many virtues along with many weaknesses. This contrast exists in other creatures, too, but it does not come close to the level displayed in humans. Animals cannot go beyond the boundaries determined for them. As they were not given free will, they have no responsibility. Devils are so unified with evil that they cannot do anything other than evil. The skills of angels are limited—limited in the sense that, unlike human beings, they cannot improve themselves. The devil is deprived of obeying, and the angel is safe from disobeying. As for human beings, they are created at equal distance to both evil and good. They have the potential to rise to the highest of the high and, conversely, go down the lowest of the low.

***

"Call to good and prevent wrong"— *amr bil ma'ruf wa nahy an al munkar*. Depending on the translations within the Qur'anic contexts, "calling to good" may be rendered as promoting the right, just, honorable, righteous behavior, and virtue; whereas "preventing wrong" is forbidding what is evil, dishonorable, and vice. The Qur'an urges believers to embrace this duty individually and collectively and praises them when they practice this obligation (Al 'Imran 3:104, 110).

The word *ma'ruf* has several meanings, like well-known, universally accepted; that which is good, beneficial; and fairness, equity, and equitableness. It is anything that has been recognized and approved by reason and moral values. *Munkar* refers to all that is denied, denounced, and abhorred, as well as injustice, immoral behavior, and vice.

This duty is meant to encourage righteous behavior and discourage immorality and aims to remove oppression from society and instead establish justice. It should, ideally, be the distinguishing trait of a Muslim community as it applies to the moral, social, political, and economic facets of life.

"Calling to good and preventing wrong" can be classified as a duty in the framework of teaching others about faith (*tabligh*). Literally meaning "to reach out" or "to convey," tabligh is directed to raise the consciousness among people about their responsibility towards religion. It disseminates knowledge about living one's faith in a principled way. Therefore, any discourse, or any act, that conveys, communicates, reminds, promotes, or publishes the teachings and commands of Allah ﷻ (*subhanahu wa ta'ala*) to the unknowing—or to the less informed—or any discourse or act, that discourages or prevents people from being wrong, unjust, or evil, comes under the meaning of this word, *tabligh*.

Rooted deeply in the Qur'an, hadith, and commentaries of notable scholars, the book in your hands is a precious resource to comprehend the context and dynamics that make spiritual mentoring and guidance an important part of a faithful life. The content of the book consists of transcripts of a series of sermons M. Fethullah Gülen delivered early in his career as a preacher. While presenting extensive commentary based on examples from the time of Prophet Muhammad, peace be upon him, and Rightly Guided Caliphs, Gülen does so with awareness of the realities of the modern era, especially with regards to being free from political interests and keeping the scope as wide as possible so to embrace the whole of humanity. The book supports the idea that spiritual mentoring and guidance is an important duty and highlights some principles mentors should take into consideration. While being an essential reference for mentors and counselors in the Muslim community, the book offers many universal principles that all faith communities can benefit from and refer to in their services.

Chapter 1

Understanding the Call

1.1. The purpose of our existence

"Calling to good and preventing wrong" is a path that leads to the purpose of creation and goal of our existence. Allah ﷻ created this palace-like universe for us to accomplish this purpose, and He assigned us—humanity—as His vicegerent for this mission. Prophets were sent for the same purpose: to convey the will and guidance of the Creator so that we humans attain peace through conscientious and loving submission. This was the mission of all Prophets and Messengers. It is the same fundamental faith that was revealed to all of them, starting from Adam (pbuh), who was the first human and the first Prophet.

When the children of Adam first opened their eyes to this life, they met a father, who had been already a Prophet teaching good and forbidding evil. This is how the story of human life began: with the mission of Prophethood. The tree of this mission would eventually produce its ultimate fruit: Prophet Muhammad ﷺ, who was in fact the original seed, which sprouted into the tree itself. He was the Sultan of the two worlds, for whom the whole universe was created, and his goal was to convey the Divine message. "Calling to good and preventing wrong" is always at the heart of the message communicated by the Prophets, and conveying this message is therefore the most significant and sublime task anyone can ever be charged with.

Adam (pbuh) was a Messenger father, who was like Polaris, a guiding star for his children. They all witnessed that Adam's eyes were constantly on the heavenly realms, that he was enthusiastically expecting to receive—and thus to fulfill—the Divine orders. They saw that he trembled in awe and bent double under the heavy burden of his mission and the responsibility of the messages received. They saw him preoccupied with the realms beyond and that his lips constantly moved and shivered with prayers. Adam (pbuh) was indeed the first human and the first Prophet, who undertook the mission of "calling to good and preventing wrong," and this mission was not unique to him and did not come to an end after him. The mission was taken over and continued by all Prophets who succeeded him.

Humanity has always needed Prophets and the Divine Message, for time and events incessantly erode and consume all the goodness and virtues in people. The Qur'an points to the fact that hearts are inclined to darken and harden at times when no renewal and reformation takes place. Darkening hearts cause visions to blur, results in dizziness, unsteadiness, loss of balance, slipping off the track, and eventually being led astray. As Allah ﷻ knows all this with His All-encompassing knowledge and as His Mercy surpasses His wrath, He sent Prophets, one after the other, all of whom enjoined good and forbade evil in accordance with the circumstances of the era.

Adam (pbuh) used up his entire lifetime for this aim and advised his children to do what is good and to avoid evil. His message continued to be observed for a certain time after his death. As the resonance and reverberations of his communication began to fade out, Allah ﷻ assigned some of Adam's noble children with Messengership. They all successfully fulfilled their mission, and each of them honored this world. Just like the sun, as one Prophet set off for the horizon, another rose after a while, illuminating us all. In between the setting and rising of each sun, humanity's sky was covered with darkness. Their departure from this world was followed by the arrival of darkness, which subsequently brought an abandonment of virtue and faith. Although many saints illuminated here and there like stars at night, it was impossible for them to provide the light expected from the sun.

Then Nuh (Noah) came, peace be upon him. Humanity heard his astounding message, which fitted his nobility. He was one of the leading prophets (*ulu'l azm*). Nuh said: "I deliver to you the messages of my Lord, and I offer you good advice and I know from Allah what you do not know" (Al-A'raf 7:62). What he meant, as it were, was this: Those who listen to me, heed my words, and board my ark, will be saved. This survival and salvation will take place both physically and spiritually. The ship floating on the sea will save your physical existence. If you attach yourselves to me with your heart and pay heed to my message, you will be saved from drowning in the huge waves of this life and the other, and you will reach peace. Otherwise, you will perish and be wasted both physically and spiritually. For almost a thousand years, Nuh advised and warned his people.

Prophet Hud (pbuh) took over the mission after Nuh. He, too, said, "I deliver to you the messages of my Lord and I am a faithful adviser to you" (Al-A'raf 7:68). He invited humanity to act in accordance with the aim of their creation.

Humanity is created to know Allah ﷻ and to feel that knowledge in their conscience. Prophets came one after the other to remind their communities of this purpose and to enable them to attain this spiritual knowledge. So did Prophet Hud and all the messengers that followed him afterwards.

Whenever the effects of the words of the preceding Prophet were erased from peoples' minds and hearts, humanity then began to falter in morality and to experience greater tremors and convulsions in their souls. Spiritual lives became like an arid desert that lacked the breezes of exhilaration and awareness that Allah ﷻ mercifully sends unto them. Humanity was in such a dry phase of their existence when Prophet Ibrahim (Abraham), the father of the Prophets, was sent.

Not surprisingly, Prophet Ibrahim, peace be upon him, was again not an exception to the rule. He approached his people with the reviving breath of "calling to good and preventing wrong." Wherever he saw a few people, he approached them and conveyed to them the Truth, Allah's Message ﷻ. Those who listened to him and took heed of what he communicated climbed the ranks of spirituality and virtue and always stayed at those peaks.

Not long after he was gone, his community started to gradually descend and degenerate from those peaks. They started to lose the qualities and virtues they had acquired. They regressed to an obstinate and materialistic mentality. They ignored and neglected the metaphysical aspects of reality, for they only believed what they could immediately see and experience—a disaster which one can certainly draw parallels to in this century.

The Nile delta was drowning in a similar vortex when Prophet Musa (Moses) (peace be upon him) emerged in Egypt. He was charged with the task of "calling to good and preventing wrong" just as the other Prophets who preceded Him. He was appointed to deal with an obstinate people. He took on this high mission and set about helping and elevating them. He had been successful in doing this to a certain degree. Although the people he was dealing with would not easily listen to reason, thanks to his ceaseless and sincere efforts day and night, he witnessed many improvements in society and was indeed able to reap the fruits of his "calling to good and preventing wrong" in his lifetime.

Being a Messenger of Allah ﷻ is not easy. Nor are teaching, guiding, and elevating people to the highest level of humanity, morality, and spirituality. "Calling to good and preventing wrong" is a difficult and demanding mission. Some people heeded the warnings of the Prophets and strove to deepen their connections with Allah ﷻ and thus refrain from committing evil. However, many others did not listen and retaliated with resistance, persecution, hatred, and even violence, because they perceived the Prophets' mission as a threat to their ways and means of life, traditions, interests, and indulgences. That is why many of the Prophets were martyred. Prophet Zechariah, peace be upon him, was cut into two with a handsaw for pursuing his purpose in life. So was Prophet Yahya (John), peace be upon him: he was martyred while trying to fulfill his mission. As a matter of fact, the cross built to crucify Prophet Isa (Jesus), peace be upon him, was for such a heinous purpose, too.

The trials and tribulations Prophet Muhammad ﷺ faced were beyond comparison. He suffered many periods of pain and torment from his oppressors. "O Aisha, I suffered a lot at the hands of your people"[1] he is recorded to have said once to his beloved wife. These words were from the broken heart of a grieved Prophet. Make an imaginary journey through history and visit every Prophet, and you will hear the same words from their hearts. "I suffered a lot at the hands of your people" they would say—be it Adam, Nuh, or Hud, peace be upon them all—to their children. This must be the unchanging destiny of those who fulfill the task of "calling to good and preventing wrong."

The fate of the blessed ones who devoted their lives to this mission after Prophet Muhammad ﷺ was no different. They sacrificed as much as they could in order to chase this heavenly aim, and in return were consistently met with similar hatred and disgust. This is essentially an unchanging destiny, to varying degrees, of the person who embarks upon this mission. Scorn and bile are, unfortunately, no surprise for a person that follows behind the prophets of Allah ﷻ. Here are the words overflowing from the broken heart of Bediüzzaman Said Nursi (d. 1960), one of those blessed ones, echoing his predecessors who had to go through similar sufferings:

"*In my whole eighty-something years of life I have known nothing of worldly pleasure. My life happened to pass on battlefields, in the prisons of foreign lands, or in the prisons and courts of my homeland. I know of no pain or torment I have not suffered. I have been treated like a slayer in the courts martial; I have been sent to exile from one town to another. My months passed in solitary confinement in my country's prisons. I was poisoned countless times, got insulted in all possible ways. On occasions, I preferred death over life a thousand more times. If my religion had not forbidden me from committing suicide, maybe Said would have already been rotted and vanished under the ground by now.*"[2]

My purpose in bringing examples from such a broad spectrum, from Prophet Adam to Prophet Muhammad (peace be upon them all), is to urge the reader to contemplate on the honor, supremacy, and reward of the task of "calling to good and preventing wrong." Every step taken on this way enables the person to acquire the merit of being an heir to the Prophet, for this was primarily the duty of all Prophets. Everyone who takes the step on this way can be considered, as it were, to have assumed this duty and therefore is blessed with a Divine favor. Their reward will be in accordance with their intentions and status of spiritual standing.

Every effort devoted to calling to good and preventing wrong brings rewards as much as an inheritor of a Prophetic mission is entitled to. For, this is primarily the duty of Prophets. Since this sacred duty is the mission of the Prophets and since all the Prophets were a perfect model of rectitude and were absolutely on the straight path with their whole being, then those who fulfill this duty of "calling to good and preventing wrong" would be considered as upright, at least in the context of this mission.

Furthermore, fulfilling this duty as is expected can also serve as a guarantee for believers in their faith. Believers can ensure their survival, both individually and collectively, as long as they teach others about Allah ﷻ and His Message. Believers need to speak up to injustice, should not grow attached to this worldly life and its corporal pleasures, nor should they drown in the fear of death. It is important for their survival to adopt the understanding, commitment, and sincerity of the Companions of Prophet Muhammad ﷺ and assume this sacred duty to be the aim of their lives. These are necessary for a person to exist and remain a believer. What a shame are the days spent lacking in such duty and pursuits. In fact, each believer should be concerned with living in a society where this duty is not fulfilled, and they should seek refuge in Allah ﷻ from such deprivation.

While performing this task, the person will have the opportunity to put into practice what they believe in, as well as uphold and defend what is paramount in life—and thus the faith they have will avoid being just theoretical. Islam is a religion of practice and commitment; it is not only an ideational and spiritual conviction. If it is not acted upon and lived on a daily basis, it can hardly be understood and appreciated. A believer who centers everything on the faith and the conveying of Allah's ﷻ messages to other people ought to plan all daily activities accordingly.

Islam requires the preservation of five necessities to ensure individual and social welfare in this life and the hereafter. They are preservation of religion, life, intellect, lineage, and wealth. Among these five essentials that must be protected, religion is the one that comes first for a believer. The believer is required to protect their honor, chastity, property, wealth, and life. Yet, they must protect their religion foremost. Doing so is regarded as the sign of the importance they attach to their religion. The most outstanding picture showing the degree and greatness of the individual's relationship to Allah ﷻ is the efforts and attempts they make to protect their religion. Besides, it should be remembered that the person who cannot protect their religion cannot protect the other four essentials cited above, either. This is one of the most appropriate and exemplary lessons history has taught us.

Allah ﷻ created us so that we may learn about Him, strengthen our relationship with Him, and share our knowledge and experiences with others. This is the Divine purpose of our creation. Acting in accordance with this purpose will make both our world and afterlife prosperous. Otherwise, failing to do so will likely result in the failure of our communities and society. We will suffer and be pushed into the midst of mischief and malice, Allah ﷻ forbid.

Let me illustrate this with a hadith narrated by the Companions Abu Ya'la and Ibn Abi'd-Dunya. One day, the Companions were sitting around Prophet Muhammad ﷺ when he spoke of a time when the duty of spiritual guidance would not be properly fulfilled. The Messenger ﷺ asked, *"What is to become of you on that day when the women rebel and rush out into the streets immodestly and unrestrainedly, when the evils spread out everywhere and telling the truth is avoided?"*

The Companions were horrified to hear these words since they were unable to believe in the possibility of such a thing. They believed that these kinds of evils would not spread within the society even if one single believer remained. They asked: *"Will these really happen, O Messenger of Allah?"*

The Prophet said: *"I swear in the Name of Allah ﷻ the Omnipotent, the keeper of my soul, that even worse will happen."*

"What is worse than that, O Messenger of Allah ﷻ?" asked the Companions, hardly able to think and speak properly due to the shock of the situation.

The Prophet, the Glory of Mankind, replied: *"Only if you knew what would become of you on that day when you will see all that is evil as good and all that is good as evil!"*

This hadith is worth examining since it is reflective of the world that many societies find themselves in today. What it underlines is that virtue and morality will essentially become reversed, and what is generally considered to be good and evil, both by religious and societal standards, will be switched. That is, that the good will be considered evil, and the evil will be considered good; that debauchery, vice, and adultery will not be discouraged but promoted; that anarchy, chaos, and terrorism will be supported and will be rampant; that the faith and the Qur'an will be belittled, mocked and those who believe in Allah ﷻ will be despised;

that corruption and vice will be protected by governmental regulations and states will make laws to protect what is evil; and that truths concerning religion will be treated as backward, obsolete, and reactionary. This is what is meant by values turning upside down. People in this century have gone through many such times severely. I believe that this trend will continue, and perhaps accelerate, unless we act to alter its course by performing our duty of "calling to good and preventing wrong." Otherwise, it is certain that insult, humiliation, and degradation will replace human honor, dignity, and values. If the laws of innate nature are broken, then the outcome is inevitable, and people should know how to endure it. This has always been the case, and it is not sensible to expect otherwise. That is why the Prophet's Companions, who could not accept this in their conscience, asked again in surprise:

"Will this happen, too, O Messenger of Allah ﷺ, namely, will the good be forbidden and will the evil be enjoined?"

The Messenger ﷺ replied, *"Even worse will happen!"*

"What is even worse than that, O Messenger of Allah ﷺ?"

"Shame on you on the day when you keep quiet face-to-face with the evil and you encourage it personally!"

In other words, it is a tragedy when we neglect our families and leave them to themselves. It becomes even worse when we encourage them to evil with our manners, words, and behaviors. Worst of all is when we cause our future generations to forget Allah ﷻ and remove the Prophet from their hearts.

The Companions were extremely surprised, weak at the knees, and hardly able to breathe. In a trembling and exhausted voice, they asked:

"Will this happen, too, O Messenger of Allah ﷺ?"

"Yes, even worse will happen." At this very moment, the Messenger swore by Allah ﷻ and narrated from Him the following words: *"By My Might and Majesty, I will disperse mischief of all kinds in a society that becomes like this."*[3]

Allah's Messenger ﷺ was miraculously expressing what it would cost the believers in the future if this important duty was not comprehended. In fact, we have such a responsibility, too. In the most sensitive part of our heart, there is the pain and grief of the weight of responsibility that has been constant for several centuries. There is no doubt that the only way to relieve this pain and grief is to comprehend and perform this task of Prophets all together as the Muslim community, as an *ummah*.

1.2. The need for conveying the message and benefits

Today, there is a greater need to call people to good and prevent wrong than at any other time. Since the door to Messengership was sealed with Prophet Muhammad ﷺ, people have gradually distanced themselves from the Divine message. It can be argued that the level of disbelief and spirit of rebellion in our age are as alarming as those experienced in all past ages combined. This is why conveying the message falls now on people everywhere.

It is very likely that those undertaking this blessed duty today may experience more troubles and pains than the people of former ages. We hope that these hard conditions will make the spiritual mentors and guides of today surpass their predecessors, be rewarded more generously, and earn a rank just behind the Prophet's Companions. As we hope for such a status for those undertaking this duty, this is not meant to fall into an error of self-admiration. In the words of Bediüzzaman, "The carnal soul is lower than all; the duty is higher than all." Besides, Allah's ﷻ favor is received by human beings in proportion with their needs. When Allah's ﷻ bestowals are distributed among human beings, its abundance is usually in inverse proportion with the person's power or competency. Allah ﷻ helps and shows more mercy towards the one who is weaker and more helpless.

The sins we are exposed to by sight and other senses have penetrated into our hearts, so much so that we feel paralyzed. Our nights long for spiritual excitement and our prayer rugs long for tears shed in awe of and loyalty to the Creator. We are in a cadaver-like state, deprived of love and affection; what other disaster than this should we anticipate? The disaster worse than this could be to go down the path Satan went—may Allah ﷻ forbid. In our age, we are so intermingled with sins that if we were given the ability to see the inner aspect of things and thus could observe our own spiritual character, we would be the first ones to run away from what we saw.

Allah ﷻ entrusted us the duty of "calling to good and preventing wrong" although we are generally so feeble and decrepit. This is simply because of our need for mercy. We are extremely small, weak, powerless, and fallible, whereas Allah ﷻ is Most High and Merciful. Even if we thanked Allah ﷻ in return for His endless mercy and compassion and glorified Him with praise thousands of times in good conscience, it would never be enough.

In our age, everything in terms of spirituality and the soul has been shaken up and collapsed. The eyes have been eclipsed, the views have become blurred, and the moral strength has been exhausted. Yet still, the voice and breath of our Prophet Muhammad ﷺ is still being heard, though as a whisper to some, and the echo of what he said centuries ago transcends time and space to reach us. This can be explained through nothing but Allah's ﷻ infinite mercy, for which we should be thankful. This can be possible by filling our souls with the reviving breaths of the Divine.

Sadi of Shiraz wrote this for the Prophet: "*How lucky is the people who have You as the captain of their boat. How lucky is the community of the faithful who is supported by You.*" Yes, it is true that we are on a rescue ship and the captain of it is Prophet Muhammad ﷺ, the sultan of the universe. Today, our Captain is speaking to us once more and wants his crew to come together: "Those who get on this ship will be saved."

I wonder if we will hear this call and respond to it affirmatively.

***

Let's now look at some verses of the Qur'an and see how Muslims are charged with this duty and what rewards await, in this world and the next, if this duty is properly performed. Allah ﷻ said:

وَلْتَكُنْ مِنْكُمْ اُمَّةٌ يَدْعُونَ اِلَى الْخَيْرِ وَيَأْمُرُونَ بِالْمَعْرُوفِ وَيَنْهَوْنَ عَنِ الْمُنْكَرِ
وَاُولٰٓئِكَ هُمُ الْمُفْلِحُونَ

"*Let there arise out of you a band of people inviting to all that is good, enjoining what is right, and forbidding what is wrong: They are the ones to attain felicity*" (Al 'Imran 3:104). There should always be a community among you who will perform the duty of "calling to good and preventing wrong," show people what is right—a community so upright that should they encounter an evil, they turn away from it as if from a venomous snake. In other words, they should be a guiding star for their society. They should be like a lighthouse by which people could navigate their ship in the ocean of social life. All other destinations and navigations should be checked by their moral status so that deviations and straying from the truth are minimized. This community of guidance should be so motivated to do this task that those who look at them will see a personified statue of "calling to good and preventing wrong." Only when they are so determined, will their message be convincing. A society without such a determined and upright community cannot find its direction until one arises from among them.

The Qur'an states:

وَمَا كَانَ رَبُّكَ لِيُهْلِكَ الْقُرٰى بِظُلْمٍ وَاَهْلُهَا مُصْلِحُونَ

"*And it has never been the way of your Lord to destroy the townships unjustly while their people were righteous (dedicated to continuous self-reform and setting things right in the society)*" (Hud 11:117). This means, as it were, if there is somewhere a community that calls people to good and prevents wrong, Allah ﷻ guarantees that He will protect the people in that region from all earthly and heavenly disasters. This is a guarantee that cannot be given by anybody else but Him.

Relying on this guarantee in the Qur'an—as well as what many outstanding personages who have my full trust have said on this matter—and upon the relevant words of all the Prophets and saints, I'd say that Allah ﷻ does not send any disasters or calamities to a place where the duty of "calling to good and preventing wrong" is fulfilled. Even if the society deserves such a punishment, that disaster and calamity may be called off for the sake of that community because the hearts of the members of that community are always connected with Allah ﷻ. They dedicate every moment of their lives to this duty. They are sorrowful and tearful on behalf of their people. The pain of their sorrow and grief hit their brain and they always writhe in pain. They are always preoccupied with thoughts like "Who can I speak to about Him? Where and how can I find such persons?" This thought is fixed in their mind during their daily routines, while eating, drinking, sleeping, and waking up. Their existence has almost become one with this lofty idea.

As long as such resolute voluntary servants of the truth are in a society, we can hope for the mercy of Allah ﷻ and that they will be safe from all earthly and heavenly disasters and calamities. If we want to be safe from the earthly and heavenly disasters and calamities, then we must immediately start performing our duty, which is the reason for and aim of our creation. Conversely, we can speculate that calamities are hitting our society perhaps because we have abandoned our duty to call people to good and prevent wrong. By fulfilling this duty, then we can hope to save our society from disasters and calamities. No other worship or prayer calls for protection for our society. Allah ﷻ may destroy and ruin a person or a society while they are praying, circumambulating the Ka'ba, or continuously saying prescribed daily prayers and recitations. However, if somewhere a dozen people are as sorrowful and tearful as mentioned above and sincerely performing their duty, we hope that Allah ﷻ renders this place secure.

In some sources outside of mainstream hadith scholarship (Israiliyyat), it is mentioned that when the people of the Prophet Lut (Lot) (pbuh)—the people of Sodom and Gomorrah—were destroyed, there were among them many devout and ascetic people who were spending their night praying and their day fasting, but they were not performing the duty of calling people to good and preventing wrong. Again, when the people of al-Ayka of the Prophet Shu'aib (pbuh)—Jethro—were destroyed, perhaps many of them were in worship and perhaps even fasting. However, we do not know a single example in history in which a nation was destroyed although there was a group among them which performed the duty of calling to good and forbidding evil.

We can consider the reality of spiritual guidance and the need for it on earth from the perspective that it is a requirement of humans being Allah's ﷻ vicegerent on earth. Allah enabled the human being to interfere in things and bestowed them with a willpower from His own. The "self" and "ego" exist only in the human being. Thus, with these qualities, the human being tries to understand the Divine through Allah's ﷻ beautiful Names and Attributes as they manifest in various forms in the universe. This is how we attain an understanding of our own real identity. The ego and the sense of ownership that give us a sense of freedom serve as a unit of measurement by way of which we can draw suppositional lines and make connections between ourselves and the Divine; this is how we can perceive and understand Allah Almighty ﷻ.

The fact that humans were given such distinctive qualities seems to mean that we were created to be a caliph (vicegerent) from the beginning. Allah ﷻ addressed His angels, saying, "I will create a caliph on the earth..." and then created Adam, the father of humanity, as His representative. He gave humanity authority over other things. A representative cannot exceed the limits determined by the person they represent. The things humans were expected to do were determined and fixed by the Divine commands communicated by Prophets. As long as humans act in accordance with those commands, they will have performed their representation properly and perfectly.

The following *mursal* hadith[1] narrated by Hasan al-Basri illuminates this issue: "*Whoever performs the duty of 'calling to good, preventing wrong' is the vicegerent of Allah, of the Prophet, and of the Book of Allah* ﷻ."[4]

It is a duty for each and everyone to know Allah ﷻ, to make Him known, to understand His message, and teach about Him and His Message, and to show with one's behaviors that we all belong to Him. Likewise, it is also the duty for us to understand and teach others about the Messenger ﷺ and the Qur'an. Practicing the principles that Allah ﷻ and His Messenger ﷺ preached and allowing for them to be practiced are also part of this duty. These duties are also the raison d'être of humanity's creation. The human being will have done their duty as much as they perform "calling to good, preventing wrong." These are each a means that enables the human being to reach Allah's ﷻ approval step by step.

According to a report by Durrah bint Abu Lahab, when one day a man asked the qualities of the best amongst people, the Prophet said, "*the one who calls people to good and prevents wrong the most*"—as well as those who "*read the most,*" "*[are] Allah-fearing the most,*" and "*strengthen the ties of kinship the most.*"[5] We may expand on this hadith in the following way: The most beneficial humans are the ones who are always involved in calling to good and spreading the goodness, who bear the burden of such a duty in heart and mind day and night. The best are those who prevent wrong and strive to prevent it from spreading. They always cherish such lofty ideals in their hearts, fear Allah ﷻ very much, lead a life in synthesis and accord with the natural laws of creation and miraculous teachings of the Qur'an—i.e., those who look at things and

1 A saying of the Prophet (hadith) reported by a Successor (the generation of Tabiun after the Sahaba, the Prophet's friends) but without naming a Sahabi. Such reports are acceptable by *ahl al-Sunna* (the Sunni scholars) as they accept all Sahaba as reliable, so their names do not need to be mentioned in a report.

events from the perspective of the Qur'an. They are the ones who remember family, strengthen the ties of kinship, and show concern for people and approach them with compassion. All of these constitute the most important duties of believers.

If we claim that we have only the best intentions and interests in our hearts towards others, if we claim that we feel and nurture only goodwill and compassion for others, the best way to show this is by fulfilling our responsibilities and duties towards them. Therefore, the most valid and vital thing to do for the whole humanity is "call them to good and prevent evil."

Besides, whoever does this duty will be appraised and honored by Allah ﷻ, as stated in the Qur'an:

لَيْسُوا سَوَآءً مِنْ اَهْلِ الْكِتَابِ اُمَّةٌ قَآئِمَةٌ يَتْلُونَ اٰيَاتِ اللّٰهِ اٰنَآءَ الَّيْلِ وَهُمْ يَسْجُدُونَ يُؤْمِنُونَ بِاللّٰهِ وَالْيَوْمِ الْاٰخِرِ وَيَأْمُرُونَ بِالْمَعْرُوفِ وَيَنْهَوْنَ عَنِ الْمُنْكَرِ وَيُسَارِعُونَ فِي الْخَيْرَاتِ وَاُولٰٓئِكَ مِنَ الصَّالِحِينَ

But they are not all alike. There are some among the People of the Book who are upright, who recite Allah's revelations during the night, who bow down in worship. They believe in Allah and the Last Day, and they promote what is right and forbid what is wrong and hasten to good deeds. And those are among the righteous. (Al 'Imran 3:113-114)

This means that whoever performs this duty, and also believes in Allah ﷻ and in the Day of Judgment, is honored by the Almighty. We are filled with hope relying on this verse and others similar to it.

Humanity today does not need harsh words, shouting, coercion, or violence; they need compassion, love, friendliness, kind words, and a soft voice. With compassion will you approach everyone; you will feel in your soul the reverberations of the pain they feel in their soul. You will share in their sorrows as if they were yours. This is what is expected from us today. As much as, and so long as, this is realized, the most important and the long-awaited task of all humanity will have been fulfilled and accomplished.

A surprising number of people in the East and West are currently embracing faith. One can also observe many people returning to religion around the world. Mosques and prayer rugs which were abandoned for so long currently share the exhilaration of the glorious days of the past with the return of many worshippers. If this is so today, then we can be hopeful of many hearts still beating with compassion. Attitudes and actions causing hatred were of no use or benefit yesterday, and nor will they be today or tomorrow.

I have heard of and listened to many individuals who re-embraced the faith of Islam. Back in the sixties and seventies, Turkey, my homeland, was in a turmoil of ideological fights that claimed thousands of lives. Many of those involved in the anarchy later said, *"Thank Allah ﷻ that we were not killed during all that fighting; otherwise, both our world and afterlife would have been ruined."* Had they been killed then, as disbelievers, they would not today be experiencing the inner contentment and the spiritual pleasures faith provides for them.

One story told from the early Islamic period is about a Muslim who—when he was still a pagan—had killed another Muslim. One day, after he embraced Islam, another Muslim reproached him because of that murder. In his response to this reproach, the story goes, he pointed to the importance of faith and how condemned he would have been if he was the one who got killed in that encounter when he was still a pagan, without faith.

Essentially, if you could go to a certain era of the history and listen to people who saved themselves from anarchy and violence to become peaceful observant believers later, you would hear the same voice, the same words. I really wonder what those who tried to solve the problems only with brute force would say if they saw those old criminals being reformed, peaceful, and crying on their prayer rugs today. To further clarify this line of thought, an authentic example from the Age of Happiness would be appropriate here.

Amr ibn al-As was a Companion who lived a long and prolific life. On his deathbed, he felt very anxious and almost ruined it. His son Abdullah, one of the scholars of the Muslim community, said to this ex-soldier and political genius: *"Father, you used to be displeased to see people who had the anxiety of death; you used to get angry towards them. Now, I see that you have the same kind of anxiety..."*

Amr ibn al-As replied as follows:

"There are three important periods in my life, which make me have various feelings. The first period of my life passed in disbelief. I did many evil things to the Messenger of Allah ﷺ and believers. I opposed them every-

where and every time I could. They migrated to Abyssinia, and I followed them and disturbed them even there. I opposed many Muslims in many battles. Many of my friends who fought against Muslims died in disbelief. Yet, Allah ☙ protected me and guided me into the true faith. Thus, I felt grateful and thanked to my Lord day and night for not having died at that time.

"In the second period of my life, I was always with the Messenger of Allah □; I never left Him. I lived a pure life in this period. Many Companions died while in this purity and sincerity, but I did not. I always lamented this and said, 'I wish I had died in this period.'

"The third period of my life was when the Messenger of Allah ☙ was not among us anymore; he passed away to his abode in the presence of Allah ☙, the Highest of all. Without him, we tried to find solutions to problems by ourselves. In this period, I got involved in many events disturbing my conscience, and death came to me in such a period. That's why I am anxious."[6]

Today, we witness many people like Amr ibn al-As, who are thankful for not having died earlier in their lives when they were in a state of disbelief. Now, they have reached the light and turned to Allah ☙ in praise and gratitude. If we can prepare a pure life for them in their second and third periods, we will have enabled them to spend their last moments in the same spirit of gratitude, too.

There is no limit to those who want to serve endlessly—especially for those who devote themselves to the love of Allah ☙, who devote their lives to make people love Allah ☙, and who strive to eliminate the obstacles before people so that they can know Allah ☙ and attain eternal bliss. Such a duty today requires further subtleties, for the humanity of today leads a life unconnected, unrelated, indifferent to Allah ☙. Rescuing them from such a whirlpool is highly difficult. Yet, it is as esteemed and commendable as it is difficult. That extent of difficulty makes the duty more valuable and rewarding.

Imagine a desperate person struggling to keep his head above water in a deadly swamp—how difficult it would be to ask him to stay calm when he is so afraid. Not much different than this desperate man, our generations are going deeper into a whirlpool every day, and it is similarly difficult, if not more so, to give them good advice to purify their hearts and keep their connection with Allah ﷻ strong. Preserving and protecting the hearts and minds is much difficult than keeping the head above water in a swamp. However, we need to overcome this difficulty. Love, affection, compassion, empathy, and tolerance are important ways to overcome this trouble since most of the people we meet face-to-face are gaining or losing their eternal life. We want them to gain their eternal life, but they are not still aware of the seriousness of the danger they are in. Thus, they may find our efforts and zeal strange and sometimes may even get angry with us. This is why how we approach them is really important, for the consequence is about gaining or losing their eternal life. Even though they may not understand and appreciate our efforts in the first place, we must continue our efforts and counselling undeterred. This is how the Prophets, the saints, and all sincere lovers of Allah ﷻ, all of whom are the suns, moons, and stars of the sky of humanity, have always done this.

Remember how much Prophet Nuh struggled when his son refused to get on board? He was not aware that he was about to get drowned. Nuh had been shaken and sunk into a silent wail when his son was taken by the waves.[7] Today, we should feel the same zeal, enthusiasm, and sadness in view of hundreds of events of the same kind happening to children…

Remember also the pain and grief of Prophet Ibrahim, peace be upon him, when he tried to inform his idol-worshiping father about the reality of Allah ﷻ.[8] His story must absolutely be giving a message to those of us today who have devoted their lives to love.

Remember, too, the suffering of the sorrowful Prophet Muhammad ﷺ next to the deathbed of his uncle, Abu Talib, who protected the Prophet for forty years. He was kindly beseeching his uncle, *"O uncle! Say, none has the right to be worshipped other than Allah and I will be a witness for you before Allah."*[9] Today, we should always remember this incident with tenderness of heart when we want to call people to good. When the Prophet was insulted and driven away by his own people, he always responded gracefully with affection and compassion, and eventually, with affection and grace, he won.[10] His road to take billions of lives after him to eternity passes through this bridge of endurance.

This sacred duty can be assumed by heroes who devote their lives to compassion and love. It is the duty of those who give up personal pleasures so that others live and take pleasure from living. This duty is for those who cannot have the peace of mind even in Paradise unless they can show humanity the way leading there.

As one of the leading heroes and devotees of Allah ﷻ, Bediüzzaman Said Nursi put this so effectively: "*If only the faith of my nation was secure, for which I'd be ready to burn in the flames of Hell. For then, as my body burns, my heart would be like a rose garden. If I do not see the faith of my nation in safety, I would not wish Paradise for myself, either. For, it would then be like a prison for me.*"[11] This is indeed the duty of the truthful ones who said, "*O my Lord, make my body so big that I fill up Hell and no other servant of Yours enters there...*"[2]

As much as these possibly spur-of-the-moment words are very difficult to put into practice, they reveal a spirit of compassion larger than the oceans.

It is narrated that the Messenger of Allah ﷺ will prostrate himself on the Day of Judgment upon finding out that some from his followers will be taken to Hell as he will cry, "*O my people.*" This is such a compassion that it makes him forget Paradise and all its beauties and makes him beseech bitterly, in tears, for their salvation. He will not raise his head from the prostration and wail there earnestly for his people, *ummah*, until he is told, "*Raise your head! Intercede, and your intercession will be accepted!*"[12] This is the expression of the matchless compassion of the one, the greatest of all heroes of love.

It is not possible for a person to be a hero of love unless they give up their personal pleasures and worldly pursuits of happiness and unless they forget themselves and worldly interests and loves. They must do this for the sake of sympathizing with others and sharing their pain. Without being a real hero of love, it is not possible to perform the duty of "calling to good and preventing wrong," either.

1.3. The most valuable gift

On special days and occasions, we spend a lot of time and trouble to choose the best gift for friends and loved ones. As bothersome as it may sometimes be, this is a good behavior, for it reinforces our friend-

2 This is usually attributed to Abu Bakr al-Siddiq, the truthful one.

ships—especially when the gift is one that he or she will enjoy using and find meaningful.

Similarly, while interacting with people in our social circles, we should be as sensitive as when choosing the best gift, so we can offer friends and family what they need most.

In today's world, what people need most is a few good words and counselling. The most valuable gift that can be given to a person is therefore "calling to good and preventing wrong" wrapped in the garb of sincere advice and kind words. To be successful at doing so, we must know and determine exactly what the person or people we address need most or are lacking. We must diligently approach each person in a way that individually suits them best, much like how a meticulous doctor prescribes a precise dosage of medication for each patient. Otherwise, for instance, even if we give the person in need a fabulous garment but one which does not suit them, it will be dressing them with an unpleasant garment. Although this is done with a good intention and a kind act, it will not produce the desired effect.

If a person is deeply fixated on a number of ideologies, trying to elevate them to the skies would produce no positive result. Telling them about heavenly matters without addressing misconceptions and misperceptions first is one of the least helpful and fruitless courses of action. How can the twinkling stars embellish the heart mirror of a person that is already eclipsed and unable to receive the light? We must do our best to approach people from the angles that specifically interest and answer their needs so that they can use their intellect and common sense and thus experience an awakening.

Sometimes a very heartfelt plea of yours is all it takes for the other person to come to their senses and question and realize what they are lacking. I believe that there is no other gift that is as valuable as that plea, which is so full of good intentions and a sincere concern for people to succeed in both this world and the next. Such a serious concern and plea of yours, in some ways, can stop and prevent the person from all the consecutive wrongs to be committed and may lead them to the right path and direction. This promising gift, the gift of "calling to good and preventing wrong," may open further gateways before them. To me, once again, there is no greater gift that one can give to another person than such a call.

Bukhari and Muslim narrate the following event, which symbolizes the importance and worth of calling people to belief in Allah ﷻ:

The siege of Khaybar lasted for days. No positive result was obtained. The residents of Khaybar were putting up strong resistance. One day, the Messenger of Allah ﷺ said: *"Tomorrow I will give the flag to such a person that he loves Allah and His Messenger; and Allah and His Messenger love him, too."*[13]

This was such good news that nobody would be willing to forsake this honor. At other times, the Companions of the Prophet would always prefer their brothers and sisters over themselves in all matters. We know stories of when they gave the last remaining water to their friend although they knew they needed it more.[14] They could easily give up everything that they possessed for the sake of a believing brother of theirs.[15] But what was said today was the good news of the guarantee of being loved by Allah ﷻ and His Messenger ﷺ. This was not an honor to disown.

In short, everybody wanted to obtain this honor, including personalities as exceptional as Umar ibn al-Khattab. Umar, may Allah ﷻ be pleased with him, said that he never wished for a position of leadership or any duty. But he strongly desired and hoped to be given the flag that night because it would signify the guarantee of being loved by Allah ﷻ and His Messenger ﷺ.[16]

The Companions could not sleep a wink till the morning and wondered who would be granted this honor. The next morning, everybody tried to find a place somewhere at the front row for the morning prayer with the hope of being selected; the flag was going to be given to its owner after the prayer. When the Messenger of Allah ﷺ turned to the congregation, everybody was all ears, for they would hear the name of the luckiest man in the world. The excitement was at its peak, and when the time finally came, the Prophet ﷺ spoke with a voice that was as tender as it was somewhat chilling: *"Where is Ali?"*

It was all clear: Ali was the lucky one. But Ali was ill with serious pain in his eyes. Could this be a chance for another one of them? With this hope they replied to the Prophet ﷺ: *"He is lying ill over there, O Apostle of Allah!"* The Prophet called him near and put his holy fingers to his mouth and then rubbed them on Ali's eyes. Those aching eyes healed, and Ali never felt this pain again for the rest of his life.

The flag found its lucky owner. Ali took hold of the flag and set off for Khaybar. Then, he suddenly stopped and asked the Prophet ﷺ: "*O Messenger of Allah! On what basis shall I fight against them? What kind of proposal shall I offer them?*" The Sultan of the Two Worlds ﷺ answered: "*Keep your composure until you enter their region (don't fight at once). Then invite them to Islam. If they accept, they will have protected their property and family from you. Their rights regarding the Hereafter are something up to Allah. O Ali! I swear by Allah that someone's embracing the faith by means of you is more beneficial than sacrificing as many red camels as would cover the entire world in Allah's way.*"[17]

Henceforth, whenever and wherever a proper Islamic army happens to enter a battle, they must do so with this command of Allah's Messenger ﷺ in their minds and they are supposed to act in accordance with it.

In the eras long before us, the mission of "calling to good and preventing wrong" had been systematized, taking into consideration different hadiths along with the practices of the Messenger of Allah ﷺ. In other words, people who assumed the duty of disseminating Allah's ﷻ call—not the army—used to move to different places to convey the message and soften people's hearts. On many occasions, such moves gave positive outcomes, and many people embraced the faith, naturally making their country a land of Islam. At other times, when Muslims were not allowed to spread their faith and had to fight, they had to comply with the principles as outlined above. In other words, calling people to faith by peaceful means would be more rewarding to the caller than sacrificing in charity as many red camels as would cover the entire world in the way of Allah ﷻ.

In conclusion, the best gift a Muslim can offer to humanity is to perform their duty to "call to good and prevent wrong." Accomplishing this responsibility in moderation, with gentleness and tolerance under all circumstances, and without becoming weary, is the greatest and most valuable of all gifts.

1.4. Continuity

"Calling to good and preventing wrong" requires continuity and determination. The Qur'an states the following:

كُنْتُمْ خَيْرَ اُمَّةٍ اُخْرِجَتْ لِلنَّاسِ تَأْمُرُونَ بِالْمَعْرُوفِ وَتَنْهَوْنَ عَنِ الْمُنْكَرِ وَتُؤْمِنُونَ بِاللّٰهِ

"You are the best community ever brought forth among [for the good of] humankind. You enjoin what is right and forbid what is wrong and believe in Allah." (Al 'Imran 3:110)

An attentive look at the verse above will reveal the high level of Qur'anic rhetoric and also illustrate why the language of the Qur'an is miraculous, unique, and evidence of Divine authority.

The expression *"kuntum"* in Arabic refers to a "becoming." That is, the quality of being "the best community" was not always the case; you were not like that from the eternal beginning. Qualities that have existed since eternity are not lost; qualities that are acquired subsequently can be lost. Therefore, the continuity of that condition is dependent on the continuity of those qualities that were necessary for that condition in the first place.

Since "becoming the best community" is an accidental quality acquired later on, it can be lost at any given moment. The absolute goodness or benevolence cannot stem from our own being. To elucidate, we could say that there is simply no difference between the essence of ours and that of other individuals born in various parts of the world. We all are beings created from a fluid drop (At-Tariq 86-6 خُلِقَ مِنْ مَاءٍ دَافِقٍ). All human beings' origin and structure are basically the same. What makes believers "the best community" and beneficial to the world is an accidental quality—we did not always have it. Being beneficial was not a quality that came encoded with this community, nor does it mean that it cannot be lost. When the believers fulfilled certain conditions, they became beneficial. However, the fact that we became beneficial once does not guarantee that we will remain so forever. If believers abandon the conditions or prerequisites that made them beneficial, they will lose the status or the attribute they were endowed with.

In the Qur'anic verse given above, the first condition for Allah ﷻ to render us best and beneficial is fulfilling the duty of calling to good and preventing wrong. Taking into consideration its opposite sense, we may say that if you do not do this duty, you cause harm or evil and lead to some malevolence at the end. Moreover, we can relate many narrations and events from the Prophet ﷺ and his Companions confirming this meaning. I assume one of the major reasons for Muslim communities treated with some disrespect in some social platforms today must be the ramification of the negligence of this duty.

In the event that this mission is no longer being performed, then the blessings of the Qur'an cease, thoughts become inconsistent, reasoning insufficient, and remarks plain, insipid, and pointless. Lots of words, the only charm of which are being vague, are uttered but not even a single drop of reality can be found in them. In fact, these are signs that the blessings of the Divine Revelation are ceasing, and it has cascading effects upon both a society's culture and its advancement in the fields of science, the economy, and technology. Unfortunately, Muslims throughout the world have become victims of such a downfall and heavily dependent upon others in many aspects. This is the outcome of our living a life devoid of the blessing of Divine Revelations and inspirations. Periods of regression and falling backward coincide mostly with our inner deformation.

Let us turn back to our main topic. We emphasized above that the verse *"You enjoin what is right and forbid what is wrong and believe in Allah"* (Al 'Imran 3:110) points out an individual and collective-communal duty that requires continuity and consistency. This is confirmed by the following hadith:

"Whoever sees something evil (munkar) should change it with his hand. If he cannot, then with his tongue; and if he cannot do even that, then in his heart. That is the weakest of faith."[18]

"Munkar" is what is wrong, abhorred. What Muslims ought to do when confronted by *munkar* is to try to change it. How to make this "change" depends on the nature of *munkar* and the context. What falls on believers is to show effort to introduce the change and to do it consistently. Changing with the "hand" is to take action. If they cannot do so, then they ought to change it with their "tongue," i.e., by counseling verbally or in a written form. If this is not possible, either, then it is advised at least to disapprove any evil practice in their heart. This third level, denouncing evil with the heart, is the least the believer is expected to do. Anything less is not possible to consider within the fold of sound faith as it implies being complacent about, and thus working not to change, such evil behavior.

Disapproving or denouncing an evil action is like when we distance ourselves from someone we are strongly angry with in the heart.

We do not wish to be in the same community with them, nor do we share with them any of our ideas or thoughts. This is because peaceful, benevolent love and strong dislike cannot exist in the heart simultaneously. Disapproving evil in the heart helps a believer preserve their conscious and moral stand. However, let it be stressed that believers should not be content with only, or simply, denouncing what is wicked or evil from the heart but ought to work to change it with their constructive efforts, actions, or speeches, in a manner that reflects good will, care, patience, and love.

No believer can love and approve an evil behavior that is disapproved by Islam. They cannot ignore such behaviors even if they are committed by one's own people. Evil is always evil no matter who commits it. Silence implies acceptance to a degree. A believer is highly encouraged to be always conscious of, or morally alert to, the actions that are being committed around him or her and how they affect them, their families and the larger community. This is also what the verse and the hadith above indicate and make us aware and informed of.

One may take action to intervene in matters that relate to his or her close circle, say the immediate family. But this may not be possible in the outer circles of their relationship, say kin and relatives, with whom they can interact verbally. If one cannot do this, either, then he or she should review his or her emotional connection with them and not allow an internal approval for the evil they are doing. The believer may act unsympathetic, concerned, or simply not interested towards such evildoers to express their disapproval. That coldness or distancing is almost a boycott in a sense in response to those who have distanced themselves from Allah ﷻ by doing evil.

In the early periods of Islam, we find many incidents, especially during and in the aftermath of the battles, of how the Companions of the Prophet thought, spoke, and acted towards their kin and relatives who came to destroy their religion, Prophet, and fellow Companions. They are all worth stressing in terms of showing a believer's attitude towards an evil behavior and how sincere believers determined and revised their relationships with others with regards to their own attachment to, or more correctly, with regards to others' detachment from, Allah ﷻ and His Messenger ﷺ.[19]

In short, whereas believers can easily establish an interest in and relationship towards people who believe and enjoin good, they act a bit reserved towards individuals indifferent to Allah ﷻ and can hardly be friendly with those who commit and condone evil. The least a believer can do towards such evil acts is a strong dislike and denouncing the evil attributes and deeds in their heart. This disgust for evil in the heart obviously requires continuity and consistency.

There are indeed lessons to take from what the Companions did when they had to make a choice between the love of Allah ﷻ and His Messenger ﷺ and the love of people who were kin and close to them but distant to Allah ﷻ. The love of Allah ﷻ and His Messenger ﷺ should be weighty in our options. However, this is not only an issue of love, either. One should also prefer the truth and reality above all else and should strive to perform the task of calling to good and preventing evil with the hand or tongue where necessary. In the event that it is impossible to change certain behaviors with our hands or tongue, then it would be wise to revise our relationships with certain people. This could even include physically or emotionally distancing ourselves from them in the event that these relationships drag us away from what really matters most. Moreover, should an interest or concern for someone else, or anything worldly for that matter, be contrary to, or regardless of, the love of Allah ﷻ and His Messenger ﷺ, carrying on and pursuing that interest may mostly turn out stressful or unfruitful for the believer because it is self-consuming due to a psycho-spiritual dilemma.

Another aspect of the duty of "calling to good and preventing wrong" is its comprehensiveness. In other words, as the duty requires continuity and consistency, it also falls within the responsibility of the government.

The government is an organized authority taking upon itself the duty to correct the evil acts with its "hand." It is able and liable to enforce rules and regulations with its agencies or institutions against certain evil acts or vice, such as obscenity, drug or alcohol abuse, gambling, profiteering, etc. Enforcing such rules or regulations are beyond an individual's capacity and authority. The frame in which the individual can interfere has already been mentioned above. In the event that State actors do not take these responsibilities seriously, citizens may voice their disapproval with their elected officials during elections. This civic responsibility of taking part in elections and warning the actors by ballot can be deemed another aspect of "calling to good and preventing wrong."

There must be a perpetual balance of power, justice, and respect of the rule of law between citizens and their governments. One event that took place during the Age of Happiness is worth mentioning since it displays how the two forces hold each other accountable and can prevent one another from committing evil. Sa'd ibn Abi Waqqas is one of the ten blessed Companions, who were promised Paradise.[20] He was the commander-in-chief of the army that conquered Iran during the reign of Caliph Umar ibn al-Khattab. He was later appointed as the governor of the province he had conquered. After a while, people complained to Umar about a doorman Sa'd had employed and asserted that the governor must see the people without a moderator. When Umar asked them if they had any other complaint, they answered that Sa'd was not as careful as he should be while observing the principles *(rukns)* of his daily prayers.[21]

This was certainly the opinion of the complainants of that time; however it is not possible for us to accept that a companion such as Sa'd ibn Abi Waqqas was not offering his prayer according to its prescribed rules. The point though is that people should be able to influence their officials and hold them accountable while the State is simultaneously able to use its power to promote the betterment of society. That incident indicates how the people were then, and are now, entitled to continuously influence the officials without interfering in what they do. In the same way, the government has the mandate to supervise and control the acts of their citizens, too. Thus, balance and justice are preserved, and the government, along with its citizens, is prevented from wrongdoings, from committing evil acts. It is imperative that this relationship is maintained in order to establish a nation, a community, that respects the rights of its people while not standing by in the face of evil.

In the light of the criteria offered above, it is hard to say that neither the people nor their governments in the Muslim world today do their respective duties properly. This lack of or failure in duty results in people engaging in various types of immoral and unethical dealings. It also results in the government remaining indifferent to such events and even supporting or protecting them tacitly or overtly through rulings or legislative acts under different titles. Today, the evil perpetrated by State officials themselves in various countries speak volumes, even though preventing immoral dealings is supposed to be their major duty. Governments are in a position to impose sanctions to maintain authority, and they have a monopoly on the legitimate use of force. The individual cannot punish an offender, criminal, or evildoer. The individual cannot use any of the sanctions in his or her own name or will. States must uphold the law and enact justice, for if every citizen was to enact their own justice by their own will and hand, then the whole society would devolve into a state of chaos and anarchy.

From our preceding discussion, we can deduce that there are differences and limits in responsibilities that individuals and the government have when it comes to advancing the duty of calling to good and preventing wrong. The government has its limits and liabilities. In other words, within such limits or borders, only the government works, functions, or operates. The individual cannot enter or interfere there. In case of forbidding evil, interfering with the "hand" falls *only* upon the officials and agencies of the government.

As to individuals, they have a role to play, though the exact details vary. There are limits that bounds, restrains, or confines the individual from acting or interfering. Individuals are most suited to holding sincere and personal conversations with those that are near them in order to sway their hearts and minds in a more beneficial direction. For example, it is a duty, a civic responsibility, for each and every one in society, to inform others of the harm and damages caused by immoral, unethical, and unlawful acts or dealings. It is again a duty and civic responsibility for each and every one to prevent such evil acts from spreading in society and thus to protect public health and welfare, by raising awareness. Therefore, interfering with the "tongue" is a duty that falls upon all individuals, all believers. This duty is especially incumbent on all scholars and intellectuals, and a far greater responsibility falls on their shoulder as to inform, educate, and influence people through their convincing arguments and discourse. Inculcating good virtue by respected members of society, in a manner that is respectful and not imposing or patronizing, may have wide-sweeping positive influence on all citizens.

Those who are in the third situation—in other words, those who are contented with disliking and denouncing the evil acts in their heart—are only the weak, incapable, or powerless individuals. If the whole community or a nation is contented with just disliking the evil acts committed, that entire community or nation is weak, incapable, and miserable, too.

In the broadest sense, governments use their hands while individuals use their speech to promote what is right, although neither group is restricted to changing what is evil with just one method. For instance, a person is expected to inform authorities of any illegal, unlawful acts, dealings, or business taking place around them. Or, they can raise awareness so other individuals know about such illegal or unlawful business and can discourage it from taking root in the town or elsewhere; this is also forbidding evil by "hand" by an individual. All such efforts or influences go hand-in-hand to promote a society that thoroughly commands good and prevents evil.

From whichever aspect we approach the issue—whether by taking action, verbally, or disliking it in the heart—the duty continues under all circumstances regardless of which approach is used. That the believers have been fulfilling this duty for ages confirms the verse and the "continuity" or "consistency" it requires, as the implied "becoming" in the verse Al 'Imran 3:110. It is imperative that we are continuous, consistent, perseverant, and unrelenting. Especially at a time and place when authorities abandon their obligations and when this sacred duty has largely been neglected by people, then it becomes our obligation to perform this duty. Our age is not a time of coercion; thus, the duty of calling to good and preventing evil should be performed by communicating verbally and in the heart. Let us remember here Bediüzzaman Said Nursi, who taught that winning over the civilized people and gaining their hearts and minds can only be possible by convincing arguments, absolutely not by coercion.

1.5. Moral obligation

A believer performs the duty of "calling to good and preventing wrong" for two reasons: first, at a personal level for the sake of Allah ﷻ and for the attainment of His pleasure; second, at the societal level, for order and common good among people as a duty asked by Allah ﷻ.

Conveying the message and teachings of faith, and making them known to people, is a moral obligation for all believers. It is a duty to Allah ﷻ. Each believing person, male or female, is responsible for this duty and should rush to perform it as we perform the daily prayers. Especially in this day and age when our society is suffering from many social ills, and the duty of "calling to good and preventing wrong" is mostly sidelined and neglected, this duty proves more important than our own personal, individual obligations. Because, when this duty is ignored, it is not possible to perform the daily prescribed prayers, pilgrimage, almsgiving, etc., as perfectly as we should. They will not be known and performed. At times, when the good is banned and the evil is encouraged, this duty concerns and pertains to the whole community, the entire nation.

Personally, I know no other duty more sublime than this. I hold that both the world and the Hereafter of those who spend their life performing this duty will be prosperous. This is a duty that needs to be fulfilled by everyone in whatever capacity they can. Be it verbally, in the form writing, or in another way, one thing that needs to be emphasized, however, is that this duty should be performed on a voluntary basis and for the sake of Allah ﷻ only. No ulterior motives, no ideological or partisan purposes should be involved in this work. Besides, the effectuality and continuity of this work depends on purity of heart and being above politics. Carrying out this sacred duty without sincerity and good faith will not produce the objectives and expected results. Let alone producing good results here, it will bring about guilt and culpability in the Hereafter.

Those performing the duty must bear in mind that the efforts to open people's hearts to Allah should only be for the love and pleasure of Allah ﷻ and for no other aspirations. Their modus operandi should be fixed according to this principle. A hadith states to the effect that whoever strives only for Allah's ﷻ word, then that person is striving truly in the way of Allah ﷻ the Exalted.[22] Those actively participating in any charitable work, be it opening schools, student dorms, or anything else, must always have this intent as they move forward to establish such institutions.

Any institution and service to be realized should be designed to remedy new generations' weak points in regard to belief and should restore their soul in the purity of their original nature so that disbelief and unrest can be prevented from developing and spreading among us. Then all the efforts to serve the common good become a breakwater against destructive surges of disbelief, chaos, and disorder. This seems to be the most effective way to stop or mitigate storm surge effects in both thought and action.

If we do not act and provide what is needed today, we cannot prevent younger generations from falling into the predicaments of disbelief and its ensuing unrest. Many people living before us have successfully exerted their efforts to shield generations from such predicaments. If we lose what they gained, what is the use of their struggle and sacrifice? They will certainly get the reward of every single deed of theirs without any loss. If we fail to heal our generations, will the self-sacrifice of the preceding generations have a meaning? However, the way they struggled with such predicaments in the past widely differs from the struggle in our time. Today, we are to reply to them with current means and ways—with education, academic research and studies, and truthful media, etc. The past generations did what they had to, and we have to do what we have to do.

Taking today's circumstances and methods of civic responsibility and engagement into account, we must establish educational, cultural, and spiritual institutions. Places of worship and other relevant institutions will serve their original purpose: raising consciousness about Allah ﷻ and His Message; flourishing peaceful Islamic thought, culture, and civilization; nurturing love, mutual understanding, respect, peaceful coexistence, and hope; and exhilaration of worship, sound spirituality, and altruistic services. Thus, we will help new generations with their proper upbringing and education. We will adorn the youth's inner world with true Islamic spirit and consciousness. I hold that any generation lacking in moral tone can hardly achieve many positive things. Because bringing up people capable of performing the most important deeds condoned by Allah ﷻ and humanity depends on our efforts. If we can work in a systematic way, many exemplary scholars, scientists, statesmen, civil servants, spiritual leaders, and guides can be brought up in our age, too. Those roses can be brought up in our garden, too, providing that the gardener does their duty properly.

As is noted in the opening paragraph, there is another aspect of "calling to good and preventing wrong" with regard to a broad set of rules that guide Muslims in a society. This aspect concerns social and religious responsibilities. It establishes principles about business, trade, mutual rights of the individuals to be protected, rules which form the basis for relations between individuals, whether Muslim or non-Muslim, as well as between man and things which are part of creation. They are basically the means and rules to establish inner and outer peace and resolve ensuing conflicts among individuals and between the individual and the state.

Islam, like every other system, has its principles concerning all fields of life, such as trade, commerce, family, social relationships, etc. To illustrate, Islam has a certain set of ethical principles for business and economy. The Muslim has to make their commercial and economic dealings within this ethical frame. They cannot give and take usury. They cannot speculate or practice profiteering. They have to avoid all unethical behaviors protecting certain classes and doing away with middle class. They have to keep justice and balance in their business and trade as well. The Muslim cannot accept anything but what Islam accepts as a commodity. They must run their own commercial dealings and business life in this way. The duty of "calling to good and preventing wrong" involves all these and similar aspects, too. Thus, the Muslim will help eliminate, or at least minimize, usury, the black market, profiteering, and other evil acts in business and trade; the things rejected by Islam will not have the opportunity either to take root or flourish within that society.

With reference to family, Islam encourages marriage, and both the man and the woman are to consent to the marriage of their own free wills. A formal, binding contract on paper is considered integral to a religiously valid Islamic marriage. Islam considers such a marriage a blessing and source of stability and provides a foundation for family life and the healthy continuation of society. It discourages indecent relationships out of wedlock, for they are likely to destroy social bonds and thus are considered harmful to society.

Islam also has prescriptions for how family members should treat one another and what their rights and responsibilities are. The family and home are very important in Islam; it dislikes and denounces all things intending to destroy these concepts. It sees this solemnized unity essential to preventing generations from being wasted.

As we see, the believer has to try to put into practice principles prescribed by Islam both in their private life and among other individuals. They should try to eliminate, or minimize, those acts that are rejected and forbidden by Islam from their private and social lives. That is all within the fold of "calling to good and preventing wrong." When the believer fulfills this duty in all aspects of their life, they will embellish themselves along with their society with virtues, and thus a virtuous community and a prosperous nation will arise. The virtuous individual means the perfect human being, a true human being. And the society composed of these individuals—and one step forward, a world made up of these societies—are what the whole humanity is always expecting. Establishing such a world undoubtedly depends on fulfilling the duty of "calling to good and preventing wrong."

In such a world we all desire, individuals always try to be beneficial and benevolent towards one another, and nations try to make both this world and the next a paradise for their own people. This leads to what we may call a competition of virtues. In a society and world where a competition of virtues takes place, it is the concept of "we and us" not "I and me" that prevails. Thus, the dull-witted and egocentric idea such as, "After I die of thirst, it does not matter whether the world remains rainless or not"[3] will vanish forever and instead the altruistic and sublime idea that "if someone is ever to die of thirst, let me be the first"[4] will flourish; and thus, blessings will prevail everywhere. The understanding of "Let everyone be prosperous and happy first, then I can also be happy in my turn, but certainly after everybody else…" will bind individuals and also the whole society, one to another. In this way, a sense of friendship, amity, and accord will be felt everywhere. In such a society, past enmities and conflicts will hardly matter.

3 This may be considered in reference to a nihilistic indifference to whatever happens once one is gone, as in the expression generally attributed to King Louis XV of France: to *"Après moi, le deluge,"* (lit. "After me, the flood").

4 This is in reference to three Companions of the Prophet, Al-Harith ibn Hisham, Ayyash ibn Abi Rabiah and Ikrimah ibn Abu Jahl, who were severely wounded in the battlefield, and yet preferred each other for the last sip of water before each breathed their last.

Essentially, all these already exist in our system of Islamic thought that forms our spiritual structure. The more human beings understand, internalize to the point of engraving it into their soul, and practice this system of thought, the more the world will be adorned with virtues. For this to become real, it is necessary that the peoples of the world are informed and that they see these virtues put into practice first—this can be realized only by "calling to good and preventing wrong."

Today, as individuals, families, and as a whole society, we are earnestly waiting for such blessed hands to take upon and fulfill this duty.

1.6. Spiritual guidance, the individual, and society

The Messenger of Allah ﷺ defined the Muslim as *"the one from whose tongue and hand the people are safe."*[5] Muslims cannot violate others' rights with regards to their property, wealth, or honor—or in any other way. They cannot covet and menace others' lives, even it is only by looking. For instance, a person's body is inviolable; looking at private parts is forbidden unless it occurs in a marital relationship. A person being immodestly or indecently dressed is a responsibility that concerns them which makes them accountable before Allah ﷻ. However, the fact that one is dressed immodestly cannot be an excuse for a stranger to look at him or her. Can a true Muslim, who has to approach this issue in such a sensitive way, ever commit an illicit act that is a major sin? Individual mistakes have always been present in all societies; in such cases what matters is the person's intention and whether he or she keeps doing it.

However, I have come to know such young people who, if an improper sight caught their eye while out shopping for necessary goods, would give alms with their limited money hoping for forgiveness. Essentially, every Muslim is expected to be like this in terms of moral values. This reveals their credibility and dependability, as Muslims are the ones others feel safe with.

5 Bukhari, iman 4, 5; Muslim, iman 64-65. The Messenger of Allah ﷺ said: *"The believer is the one from whose tongue and hand the people are safe; the believer is the one from whom the people's lives and wealth are safe." Sunan an-Nasa'i,* The Book of Faith and its Signs, 8:47.

The true Muslim cannot touch even a single morsel belonging to someone else. If all the treasures of the world are next to them, but they belong to someone else, the true Muslim does not, and cannot, think of taking advantage of one single dime, since they are people of confidence and trust. All should be comfortable with the community of Muslims.

The opposite meaning of the hadith above points out that those who do not respect the boundaries Allah ﷻ prescribed but take their own whims, desires, and ego as their Lord are the ones whom people are not safe with. Today, humanity is right in worrying about such individuals since they do not give a feeling of security. I suppose tragic events in history are enough proof of that, and therefore require no further elaboration.

The religion of Islam adorns its adherents with virtues and expects that the Muslim's moral and spiritual structure should be positively different from that of others. The society where such virtuous Muslims live is supposed to have closed its door to all kinds of immorality and to take a stand against all kinds of *munkar* (wickedness) denounced by the religion. Low desires cannot prevail in such societies which diffuse serenity all around them. The primary duty of Muslims is to become such a society and to try to spread the ensuing goodness around the world.

It follows that, this duty must be performed by the individual in the first place, and then it must be handled in the frame of society and state. There is no doubt that a brilliant society is made and composed of spiritually enlightened and exemplary people. And such a composition attracts not only individuals but also masses and nations to itself. One example to illustrate this universal truth clearly is the event of Ashamah ibn Abjar's (d. 631) becoming Muslim. Ashamah was the Negus, al-Najashi (king), of Abyssinia, or what is now known as Ethiopia. He had a reputation for his just rule. When persecution against the Muslims increased in Mecca, Prophet Muhammad ﷺ instructed some of them to seek protection in Abyssinia so that they could worship Allah ﷻ and practice their faith in peace. In the course of time, Ashamah had the opportunity to observe them and saw how they spoke, how they behaved, as well as the light of spiritual joy on their faces and the faith in their heart. He perceived the luminous way that leads Muslims to the truth. He immediately yielded himself to the Messenger of Allah ﷺ. This was indeed the fruit of "calling to good and preventing wrong" realized in his very palace, for the Muslims themselves had already believed and were practicing first what they shared with Negus. In other words, Negus observed, was convinced, and thus admired not only the Muslims' words but also their sincere manners and virtuous personality, which formed their spiritual side.

The letter Ashamah wrote to the Messenger of Allah ﷺ was an example of court etiquette from start to end. He began his words by addressing the Prophet: "To the Messenger of Allah from Negus...." Putting the name of the person before his name was evidence that he venerated the Prophet according to the tradition of his time. The content of the letter is worth reading again and again to witness Negus's courtesy and feel his excitement in his words. Especially the following words are noteworthy: "O Messenger of Allah, if you ask, I will come at once. If you ask, I will stay here and preach Islam to my nation..."[23] On another occasion, Ashamah sorrowfully said: "I wish I had been a servant of the Messenger of Allah rather than being a sovereign king!"[24]

He was moved by the example of the Prophet's Companions and the beautiful words they had uttered. Here is how the event was narrated in reliable resources:

The early days of Islam were marked by torture, persecution, and humiliation of all kinds in Mecca. The polytheists in Mecca were determined not to accept but to eradicate Islam and the Muslims. Muslims' lives, property, honor, and dignity were not safe. Then the Messenger of Allah ﷺ gave the permission to immigrate to Abyssinia. With their arrival, Muslims were given a friendly welcome and encountered an interest much higher than they expected. Yet, the pagans of Mecca were determined to persecute them even in Abyssinia. They could not tolerate the Muslims living and practicing the religion even in a Christian Kingdom. They sent a delegation to Abyssinia to demand Muslims' extradition. The delegation was headed by Amr ibn al-As, who was a Meccan dignitary, who would later embrace Islam and be a great Companion. The delegates aimed to provoke Negus and courtiers so that they would stop sheltering the Muslims. With such an outcome, the delegates also aimed to spread utmost despair among all Muslims anywhere.

Negus Ashamah listened to the delegates at length. The disbelievers of Mecca were slandering the Muslims as much as they could and tried to impress Negus. Yet, Negus was the embodiment of munificence, benevolence, and justice. He would not expel those who took refuge in him due to such lame excuses. He clearly stated that he would not make a decision without listening to the Muslims as well. Eventually, a group of Muslims were invited to the palace. Ja'far ibn Abu Talib was leading the Muslim group. He was one of the noblest men of Mecca and the cousin of the Messenger of Allah ﷺ and the elder brother of Ali. Muslims had already chosen him as the spokesman. There was a unity and solidarity among them as if they formed one single body there. Their solidarity was quite evident from all their manners.

Those who entered the palace used to prostrate themselves according to the protocol of that time. But the Muslims did not prostrate, for Muslims would only prostrate themselves before Allah ﷻ. That made the Meccan delegation quite happy, as they assumed that Negus would get angry and dismiss them from his presence. However, Negus was a paragon of virtues as mentioned above (I wish those who claim to represent true democracy today could learn from that honorable Abyssinian ruler who lived fourteen centuries ago; then there would be a grain of truth in their claims!) Negus asked some questions to the Muslims. Ja'far answered them in the following words:

"O Negus. We used to be people of ignorance: we worshipped idols, ate carrion, committed all sorts of sins. The strong would persecute the weak. Thus we were until Allah sent us, from among ourselves, a Messenger whose good name, honesty, trustworthiness, and integrity were well known to us. He called on us to believe in the One and only Allah, and to stop worshipping all idols which we and our forefathers used to worship besides Allah."

Ja'far went on speaking and told more without hesitation. Negus was listening to him in ecstasy. Later, he asked Ja'far what the Qur'an says about Isa (Jesus) and Maryam (Mary). Ja'far recited from the Surah Maryam in awe. What was stated in the verses had deeply touched Negus, his patriarchs and courtiers. They were all in tears. Negus picked a little stick from the floor and said: "What you have just said about Jesus does not go beyond the truth by the width of this stick." He said the following historically noteworthy words: "I swear by Allah that there is no difference between what was revealed to your Prophet and what was revealed to Isa, not even as much as this stick!" Indeed, there was really no difference between them since all the revelations of the Prophets had originated from the same, Di-

vine source. Negus dismissed and sent back the disbelievers along with the presents they had brought. He assured the Muslims that they would have his full protection.[25] *Because he had observed in the Muslims great glimmerings and emanations of virtues even if for a short while, but that alone sufficed for him to accept Islam.*

An important reality to consider is that "calling to good and preventing wrong" is a duty that should be taken upon individuals first. If individuals stay away from this duty, a virtuous society can never come into existence.

Just as individuals have to protect the virtues they have gained, so do societies. As remarked above, virtues a human being attains were not eternal in the past nor will they be in the future. There is a subsequent "becoming" in this issue as explained earlier in reference to the verse Al 'Imran 3:110. The acquired virtues and benevolence require the continuity and prevalence of the conditions that render them possible in the first place. Nobody, except for the Prophets, is guaranteed on this issue. The Prophets were given this guarantee as an advance reward for their future virtues, struggle, and victory they would obtain with their own willpower. Allah ﷻ knew with His Divine knowledge—which is free from time and space—the high status Prophets would reach in the future. Therefore, apart from the Prophets, everybody, however great they are, must always work hard to maintain the high levels they attain. Otherwise, there may always be declines and losses of what has been achieved.

The virtues that "calling to good and preventing wrong" brings to the individual and the community can be protected by doing the same: "calling to good and preventing wrong." Otherwise, a gradual decline will begin, and this regression will result in the exhaustion of the society not fulfilling this duty. In order not to fall into such a situation, metaphysical consciousness and enthusiasm must always be kept alive. This is again possible with "calling to good and preventing wrong." In other words, this blessed duty is both the life itself and the condition to protect the life. For this very reason, it seems, the Messenger of Allah ﷺ stipulated the fulfilment of this duty as a condition while accepting people's oath of allegiance. Jarir ibn Abdullah al-Bajali said: "*I made an oath of allegiance to the Messenger of Allah ﷺ. He accepted my oath with the conditions that I will offer prayer perfectly, pay the Zakat (obligatory charity) regularly, and give good advice to everyone you meet.*"[26] This meant that Jarir was expected to "call people to good and prevent wrong."

This sacred duty makes the person enjoy and benefit more from the virtues of other acts of worship. For the person, who prays and is fully devoted to the duty, has already become endowed with certain virtues and able to be motivated to all kinds of other virtues. Secondly, they are doing a duty that the Prophets fulfilled and a duty that was the goal of the Prophets' lives and mission. That is why it is the heaviest, the most difficult of all tasks. Therefore, the accrued reward and benefits will naturally be higher. In the Qur'an, we find Luqman counseling his son and pointing out the heaviness of this duty:

يَا بُنَيَّ اَقِمِ الصَّلٰوةَ وَأْمُرْ بِالْمَعْرُوفِ وَانْهَ عَنِ الْمُنْكَرِ
وَاصْبِرْ عَلٰى مَٓا اَصَابَكَ اِنَّ ذٰلِكَ مِنْ عَزْمِ الْاُمُورِ

"My dear son! Establish prayer, encourage what is good and forbid what is evil, and endure patiently whatever befalls you. Surely this is a resolve to aspire to." (Luqman 31:17)

First, Luqman advises his son to observe his prayers. This is as if he means to say, "My son, someone who does not observe prayer cannot strive in the way of Allah ﷻ, either. Prayer is prerequisite for all worship being accepted by Allah ﷻ. Therefore, first of all, make this worship of yours towards Allah ﷻ properly and then with this dynamic inside you, try to spread the good and prevent the evil around you. While doing this, you will certainly be subjected to various troubles and tribulations; be determined to be patient with these, too. It is no surprise for the person striving in the way of Allah ﷻ to run into hardships, troubles, and tribulations. On the contrary, this is something anticipated by all who are striving for this cause. No exception of this has ever been experienced. This is among the great tasks only great people can cope with and the reward of which can only be reckoned by Allah ﷻ. And these great tasks will elevate the person to the level attained by the holy ones in the Hereafter. The hardships and tribulations are, as it were, by default the distinguishing feature of such great people and causes. While fulfilling the duty of calling to good and preventing wrong, the person needs patience worthy of, proper to, the great people, too."

The Messenger of Allah ﷺ pointed out the importance and heaviness of this duty in the following hadith: *"The most beneficial of my ummah are the ones who are subjected to strife and tribulations among the ignorant."*[27] Another hadith confirms this fact, too: *"The believer who is among people and endures their aggrievances wins more rewards than the one who stays away from such people and does not endure their grievances."*[6]

Staying in an unfavorable community and bearing up under the hardships in order to perform "calling to good and preventing wrong," is a higher and far more rewarding worship than staying away from everyone and devoting oneself only to the worship and prayers. If this holy duty were not more sublime than personal worship, the Messenger of Allah ﷺ would not go out of his house, would never meet and mix with any people but would always prefer to be busy with opening his heart to the manifestations coming from Allah ﷻ in seclusion. If this duty was not more auspicious than other deeds, in particular solitude and seclusion, our Prophet would not be addressed in the following way in the Surah al-Muddaththir (74:1-2): *"O you cloaked one (who has preferred solitude)! Arise and warn!"* (يَا أَيُّهَا الْمُدَّثِّرُ قُمْ فَأَنْذِرْ) The Messenger ﷺ had been put under the burden of a great mission; he had to arise from his solitude to perform the mission with resolution and courage among the people.

Religion is sincere conduct and sincere advice. Religion is "calling to good and preventing wrong." This is the command given by the Messenger of Allah ﷺ to his Companions. When he said, "Religion is good advice and sincere conduct (*an-nasihah*)," the Companions asked, "To whom (should it be directed to)?" The Messenger of Allah ﷺ answered, *"To Allah, to His Book, to His Prophet, to the public authorities of the community, and to common folk."*[28]

The believer must ceaselessly speak about the Divine; it must be their greatest concern. They will be so immersed in it that when they cannot speak about Allah ﷻ, their sleep will be interrupted, their appetite will be lost, and they will consider they have not lived that day.

Speaking about the Messenger of Allah ﷺ is another of their passions. They will tell all about his life, his accomplishments, and what he endured for the sake of his sacred mission. In this way, they will enable the believers to take the Messenger as their role model.

6 Tirmidhi, qiyamah 55; Ibn Majah, fitan 23. "'The Muslim who mixes with the people and he is patient with their harm is better than the Muslim who does not mix with the people and is not patient with their harm.'"

Likewise, they will speak about the Book of Allah ﷻ, how Allah ﷻ sent it to His Messenger ﷺ as a letter, as an invitation, and as a guidance. Allah ﷻ sent to us the Qur'an as the manual, guidebook, and lodestar so we can find our path in this worldly life. Our honor, personal dignity, and progress are all dependent on and proportional to our understanding and loyalty to His Book. We can make inferences from history in that whenever the Muslim world embraced the Qur'an, internalized it, and thus acted upon its teachings and principles, it always stayed in the peaks, and whenever the Muslim world gave it up, it regressed into disarray.

Here, I would like to note a grief of mine. It is indeed a grief because not only thinking about but also reporting it makes me cringe.

Today's Muslim is in such a condition that they cannot understand the language of the Qur'an, the Book of Allah ﷻ. Metaphorically, the Qur'an is in one valley, they are in another. Adherence to the Qur'an has turned completely into formalism. For instance, you would see people warning others not to hold the Qur'an copy in their hands lower than their belly (there is no such religious commandment; holding the Qur'an above is a sign of respect). But you would see the same people leading a life that is diametrically opposed to the principles of the Qur'an.

It is believers' ultimate responsibility to protect the Qur'an and shape their lives according to it. Outward reverence showed for the sake of formality is meaningless without abiding with it. Alas! I wish the veil of the Unseen were lifted and thus the other world became visible for once, so that everybody—including preachers, religious legal experts, writers, thinkers, readers, listeners, teachers, and students—could see the predicament of their being detached from the Qur'an in this world. However, since such a manifestation would invalidate human free will, it is contrary to the secret of their being tested in this world.

Even though I spoke of the Unseen becoming visible in order for people to see what would befall them in the Hereafter for their negligence in this world, in fact it suffices to think about it even for a short while and evaluate our current status and fate in this world. The high toll we are paying for staying away from the Qur'an is as clear as daylight. What more do we need to pay so we can reembrace the Qur'an? What other big humiliation can make us run towards the Qur'an? We must cease this living indifferently or detached from the Qur'an, and the whole Muslim community must know that the only way of salvation is the Book of Allah ﷻ. Our glorious Prophet ﷺ came to tell us this. And to the extent that people understand it, they will rise to true humanity.

Awakening others to faith makes one a shareholder in their good deeds; one can earn rewards equivalent to theirs. In other words, let's suppose that you have been instrumental in a person's decision to start a new life in which he offers his prayers, gives alms, fasts, and observes other aspects of religion. The equal amount of rewards incurred by such good deeds the person performs will also be given to you, as is noted in the heartening words of the Messenger of Allah ﷺ, the Sultan of eloquence: "*Whoever guides someone to goodness will have a reward like the one who did it.*"[29]

In addition, if the person you have guided guides another person to the right path, you will also receive rewards from this. Thus, a minor good deed performed with this sincere intention enables one to acquire such major rewards, which shows how important "calling to good and preventing wrong" is. The Messenger of Allah ﷺ expressed this fact from a different perspective: "*Whoever starts a good tradition which is followed, then for him is a reward, and the likes of their rewards of whoever follows him, there being nothing diminished from their rewards...*"[30] From this and similar hadiths, we see that rewards never change whether the guided and enlightened people are kin, relatives, or complete strangers.

Pioneering something good, starting a good tradition in terms of reviving faith in our lives and appropriating it to a larger community, will ensure our account of good deeds remains open even if we are gone. In fact, this is true for all kinds of good deeds, righteousness, benevolence, generosity, and philanthropy.

We should keep in mind that one day each and every one of us will pass away, be carried away in a coffin, and buried in a grave, covered by earth. A gravestone will mark our place. After the burial, everyone, including our parents, brothers and sisters, friends and even our most beloved ones will leave us there and go away. However, rewards originating from the good things we pioneered will come along with us in abundance to fill our grave and our next world with light. We will be dead physically, but we will continue to live until the Judgment Day thanks to the seeds we sowed while we were in this world. It has been fourteen centuries since Prophet Muhammad ﷺ passed away. Nevertheless, who on Earth is more alive than the Prophet ﷺ with his account of good deeds that is all the time open, current, and never closes? He was followed by those who have made golden contributions to human life and their faith. Millions have followed in their footsteps. They all have earned rewards to the extent they were instrumental in others' doing good work. Allah's ﷻ mercy is infinite, if only people enter the way that will lead them to that Grace and Mercy.

The Messenger of Allah ﷺ said: "*Everybody's account of deeds is closed and sealed after his death. But the* murabit*'s account of deeds goes on expanding until the Judgment Day.*"[7] Based on this and similar hadiths, the "*murabit*" is someone who devotes themselves to the way of Allah ﷻ and thinks of nothing else but their blessed duty. While on the one hand they guard the frontier of their country from all evil, on the other hand, they strive against temptations of his or her own soul. For them, sharing their inner contentment, blessings, and prosperity with others is the most important duty of their lives. Such a person's account of deeds and rewards never closes; it remains current and goes on increasing, expanding constantly.

In the Islamic history of spiritual mentoring and guidance, there have been people as such who sowed countless seeds of good deeds but passed away without seeing a single sprout, a single smile, or a pleasant outcome. But there are also people whose seeds they sowed sprouted some fifty years later and everywhere then became springlike. The rewards of all those indeed have turned their grave into an abode of light and peace. Allah ﷻ augmented their good deeds, protected these people from the trials and tribulations in the grave, and granted them with the Divine light in abundance. In other words, those people died only in terms of their bodies, but they go on living in terms of Allah's Grace

7 Tirmidhi, Fadail'l-jihad 2; Abu Dawud, jihad 15; Darimi, jihad 33. The Messenger of Allah (ﷺ) said: "The deeds of everyone who dies are sealed. Except for the one who dies guarding the frontier from the enemy, in the cause of Allah. For indeed his actions are increased for him until the Day of Judgment, and he is secure from the tribulation of the grave." And I heard the Messenger of Allah ﷺ saying: "The *mujahid* is one who strives against his own soul."

and rewards ﷻ. In fact, those people live more vividly than the so-called living people who could not perform or succeed in such a good deed.

1.7. Faith and hypocrisy

The believer is the one who sets an example of virtue representing truth in their community, starting from their nearest circle and the people closely related to them. This is the indispensable condition of being a believer and, as it were, a natural outcome of fact that other believers are safe from his or her "tongue and hand."[31]

All Muslims are, as mentioned in a hadith, like a single organism.[32] When a malfunction occurs in one of the limbs, the entire body suffers. When each limb of the body is perfect on their own, the whole body becomes perfect, too. Then, what could be more natural than the fact that believers are troubled by each other's sufferings and are complacent with their joy?

Believers really are like the limbs or organs of a body. Especially, if pain or joy concerns eternal life, how can the believer remain indifferent to their brother's or sister's going to the Heaven or Hell? That is why, it is the sine qua non quality of being a believer to perform the duty of "calling to good and preventing wrong" towards another believer:

وَالْمُؤْمِنُونَ وَالْمُؤْمِنَاتُ بَعْضُهُمْ اَوْلِيَاءُ بَعْضٍ يَأْمُرُونَ بِالْمَعْرُوفِ وَيَنْهَوْنَ عَنِ الْمُنْكَرِ وَيُقِيمُونَ الصَّلٰوةَ وَيُؤْتُونَ الزَّكٰوةَ وَيُطِيعُونَ اللّٰهَ وَرَسُولَهُ اُولٰئِكَ سَيَرْحَمُهُمُ اللّٰهُ اِنَّ اللّٰهَ عَزِيزٌ حَكِيمٌ

The believers, both men and women: they are (awliya) guardians, confidants, and helpers of one another. They enjoin and promote what is right and good, and forbid and try to prevent the evil, and they establish the Prescribed Prayer in conformity with its conditions, and pay the Prescribed Purifying Alms. They obey Allah and His Messenger. They are the ones whom Allah will treat with mercy. Surely Allah is All-Glorious with irresistible might, All-Wise (at-Taubah 9:71).

All believers, men and women, are each other's friends. And this friendship requires them to call one another to the good things Allah ﷻ approves of and to forbid the evil things Allah ﷻ disapproves of. After all, a friend cannot treat a friend in any other way.

However, believers do so only after they internalize Islam and make it an integral part of their nature. They perform their daily prayers properly, pay their alms in full, and obey Allah ﷻ and His Messenger ﷺ in all matters. When every person in the society is like this and acts this way, society automatically maintains law and order. Allah's ﷻ mercy and grace surround them with all its immensity, and the land is saturated with Divine compassion.

The hypocrites are the full opposite of the sincere believers. The Qur'an depicts the hypocrites as follows:

اَلْمُنَافِقُونَ وَالْمُنَافِقَاتُ بَعْضُهُمْ مِنْ بَعْضٍ يَأْمُرُونَ بِالْمُنْكَرِ وَيَنْهَوْنَ عَنِ الْمَعْرُوفِ
وَيَقْبِضُونَ اَيْدِيَهُمْ نَسُوا اللّٰهَ فَنَسِيَهُمْ اِنَّ الْمُنَافِقِينَ هُمُ الْفَا سِقُونَ

The hypocrites, both men and women, are all of a kind: enjoining and promoting what is evil, and forbidding and trying to prevent what is right and good; and they withhold their hands (from doing good and spending in Allah's cause). They are oblivious of Allah (with respect to faith and worship, and serving in His cause), and so He is oblivious of them (with respect to rewarding). Assuredly, the hypocrites are those who are the transgressors. (at-Taubah 9:67).

Contrary to the reference to believers in the verse 9:71, the Qur'an does not use the term "*awliya*" for hypocrites in 9:67. Hypocrites are not true friends with anyone; the only bond they build with others is self-interest. If there were to be even a shred of loss or damage to their interest, they would immediately begin to fight mercilessly amongst themselves. The verse reveals their mood with a very concise and miraculous expression and says, "*they are all of a kind*"; in other words, they are all the same unholy.

Another common attribute of the hypocrites is that *"they promote evil."* They continuously suggest evil to generations. Through publications and various means of media, they captivate people, in particular the youth. Individuals almost become addicted and bend under their heavy propaganda. Dizzy, poorly reasoned mobs and clouded masses are the pawns hypocrites always exploit. There seems to be no principle they would not compromise, nor is there any wickedness they would not try against humanity in order to maintain their interests and powers of exploitation.

Hypocrites are immediately recognized for their distinctive characteristics wherever they are in the world. For, they constantly promote evil and deter people from doing good. They put psychological pressure on the society and label everyone who wants to lead a virtuous life as backward. Those offering prayer and fasting are considered by them as fundamentalist. In their eyes, the modest clothes women wear are the most terrible signs of a lack of progress and misfortune. If you talk about loving your nation, they consider you a fascist.

All good things are *munkar*—evil—in their opinion. They are allergic to almost everything people consider to be good, righteous, and legitimate; this is a position they take out of their hypocrisy. Hypocrisy is a pit people fall into when they cannot reach integrity between how they look outside and what they truly are inside.

Hypocrites are the miserable ones who are disposed to the deepest pit of Hell:

أُولٰٓئِكَ كَالْاَنْعَامِ بَلْ هُمْ اَضَلُّ اُولٰٓئِكَ هُمُ الْغَافِلُونَ

"They are like cattle [following only their instincts], rather, even more astray; for such people are entirely heedless [of warning]." This verse (al-A'raf 7:179) is a complete picture that frames them.

Believers must protect themselves from falling into this situation by fulfilling their responsibilities. For this, they should constantly encourage each other to do good and discourage each other from evil deeds. They must fear being hypocrites in their own lives. Likewise, they should also be concerned and tremble with the fear that their friends might suffer such a fate. They should therefore keep both themselves and the community in which they live awake and vigilant. Yes, these are essential, inseparable qualities, the *sine qua non* of being believers.

For a society to establish peace, people should be very cautious about all kinds of evil acts, big or small, and should not allow them to thrive. Many small evil acts have the potential to spread like a contagious malady and, like a plague, threaten an entire community, an entire nation, and even the whole of humanity, causing them to be ruined and miserable. Social disorders have commonly arisen from the spread of such evil acts, which seemed small at their onset. When we look at history from this perspective, it is possible to see many moral and social decays whose recurrence would lead to the same fate again and again. The following hadith is very important for the historical analysis of such decays or corruption.

The Messenger of Allah ﷺ explains how the moral breakdown starts in a society with an example:

When the Children of Israel fell into decline (became deficient in religious commitment), a man among them would see his brother committing a sin, and prohibit them from it. The next day, (however) what he saw him doing would not prevent him from eating with him, drinking with him, and associating with him. So Allah ﷻ pitted their hearts against each other. … (The Messenger of Allah ﷺ was reclining, so he sat up and said) "'No, by the One in Whose Hand is my soul! Not until you take the hand of the wrong-doer and incline him toward the truth.'"[33]

Here, the situation of some of the Israelites who allowed or condoned evil is told; believers are warned about the same fate and instructed not to fall into such a situation. This warning is the wisdom in reporting this case, which can also be analyzed as follows:

A person noticed that one of his friends was doing an evil act. He did not approve of it and warned his friend. However, when his friend did the same thing again the next day, the person did not warn him this time. His friend insisted on committing the sin, but the person did not persevere in warning him. But "calling to good and preventing wrong" does require insistence and metaphysical motivation. Quite the contrary, he approached the person and ate and drank with him and maintained his close friendship and business with him. Denouncing and condemning the evil in his heart would be the last and the least sign and manifestation of his faith, he could not show even a small sign of disapproval. In time, when no one showed any disapproval, that evil spread within the community. And the Almighty set their hearts against each other and even created internal conflicts among them and thus divided them into groups. Allah ﷻ always pits the hearts of those who reject and oppose the faith, and then leads them into evil—that is, hostile competition, hypocrisy, and disorder on account of their association with their ilk.

As to the Children of Israel, they suffered many pains and were subjected to many insults from different rulers, nations, and faith groups. At an earlier time, a large number of Judeans lived a life of slavery and exile in Babylon and Egypt for centuries. They had been subject to the most disgusting tortures by Nebuchadnezzar and Cyrus and could never live in peace. The only reason why they had fallen into such a situation was that they did not "call to good and prevent wrong" among themselves, which is why the strife of separation developed in their hearts and caused them to be shaken to the core. When the Messenger of Allah ﷺ reported such a case, he warned his *ummah* (the Muslim community) that they should do the things that needed to be done from the beginning in order not to fall into the same fate and taught them to be saved from collapsing as a community.

Having come to such a point, I consider it useful to emphasize a point that can be considered tangential or insignificant to the main issue being discussed. Some of the Israelites were not able to secure an alliance and unity even in the time of the Prophet Musa (peace be upon him). So, they were always being punished. If the Jewish people today seem to be successful, as they are, this must be thanks to the alliance they have achieved, at least as seen from the outside. This alliance, which stemmed from protecting their historical values and religious dynamics, resulted in them establishing a state. If they move away from their historical values and enter into internal strife, it will be inevitable that they will experience breakdown and collapse. Yes, today's Israelites and Jews are rewarded for upholding their religion which has its origins in the heavens.

Yes, the Islamic world today is sick. It suffers from many deprivations. It is imperative that Muslims shake themselves off these deprivations and return to their own true essence. Their spirit is in disgrace, their mind is weak, and all the limbs of their collective body are in a malaise. If not treated urgently, it will get worse every day. However, when treated, the service Muslims will undertake will be the size of the entire globe. I hope that on that day, people will see that Islam is truly embracing all the earth's peoples and offering a new harmony and spirit to the world.

***

In the history of Islam, there are many incidents that prove that the duty of conveying the message and spiritual guidance are a sign and characteristic of the believer. One such incident is related to Caliph Abu Bakr. One day, Abu Bakr warned people listening to him that they were misinterpreting a verse:

"You recite the verse 'O you who believe! Your responsibility is your selves (so consider how you are faring along your own way). Those who go astray can do you no harm if you yourselves are guided' (al-Ma'idah

5:105). I heard the Messenger of Allah say, 'When the people see the wrong-doer and they do not stop him (from doing wrong), then it is soon that Allah shall envelope you in a punishment from Him.'"[34]

The above verse does not mean, "Do not bother yourself with others; you only look at your own self!" On the contrary, the verse means that one can discuss the errors, sins, deceits, and deviations of others, but he or she should not neglect themselves while doing so. So, in fact, there is an incentive to personal accounting here. Abu Bakr (radiyallahu anh), as one of those who understood this meaning best, quoted the hadith he narrated from the Messenger of Allah ﷺ as evidence for this understanding.

There are many other hadiths of the Messenger of Allah ﷺ related to this subject. I would like to point out some of them owing to the importance of the issue. In a hadith reported by Hudhayfah ibn Al-Yaman in *Tirmidhi*, Allah's Messenger ﷺ said:

"*By the One in Whose hand is my soul, you must call to good and prevent wrong, or else Allah will soon send [a common] punishment upon you all. Then, you will call upon Allah and it will not be answered for you.*"

In another hadith narrated by Ahmad ibn Hanbal, after similar statements, it is added that Allah ﷻ will set wicked ones to rule people. Then the prayer of good ones will not be accepted.[35]

The wicked ones are the disrespectful mob that do not understand or care much about human affairs and administration. They do not mind or observe the principles of religion. They are unaware of the Book and Prophet. They ridicule whatever is known to be holy or sacred. Whichever nation or state Allah ﷻ sets those wicked ones on, that nation or state can hardly be reformed any longer. Allah Almighty ﷻ postpones or delays—that is, He gives respite—but never neglects at all. He may postpone the punishment for the evil or oppression for a while, give the perpetrators respite so that they can come to their senses, repent, reform, and correct their wrongs. In case they do not, He calls them into account, and then no one can ever escape the consequences. Likewise, He may also throw back the penalty for not doing the duty of "calling to good and preventing wrong" for a while; but when it is time for the Divine Will and Decree, when the time of accounting and punishment is due, the wicked ones cannot escape.

The wicked ones coming to power is a punishment by itself for the Muslims (because the wicked ones rule the nation with hubris, brute force, and oppression, and the Muslims have deserved this because of their own negligence in all affairs and duties). In the meantime, even if the good individuals, the benefactors, fill the mosques, pray, supplicate, and beseech in tears until the morning, they will not be able to escape from the predicament until the punishment's time is over. This is a Divine law, and it will never change.

Looking into the events of the past in all aspects of life, one may infer that the picture has always been the same since time immemorial. What we see today is only one or two frames from the roll of historical recurrences. The fact that prayers, wailings, and lamentations by the Muslims are not accepted by the Supreme Court of Heaven can be explained with nothing but a sin that needs to be expiated. This sin is the neglect or failure to fulfill the sacred duty that we keep emphasizing in this work: "Calling to good and preventing wrong."

This sin is what has detached us from our Lord. "Calling to good and preventing wrong" was our raison d'être, what we were created for. This is especially true for those of us who devote ourselves to the way of Allah ❁; for whom even Paradise is not a main goal, because they are the ones who—should an opportunity arise—would consider speaking of Allah ❁ to all the other beings of Heaven over all the blessings therein. They are the ones who are so sincere and altruistic as to take the message even to the demons of Hell if it was possible. If these devoted ones neglect this very important duty, it would mean that a visa has been issued for catastrophic events and sufferings to befall us. Then, if there is anything left to be done, it is prayer. Yet, only Allah ❁ knows if they would work, for the benefit of the supplications is up to Allah ❁. Being already subjected or susceptible to such a situation means being already stuck in complete destruction. Such a day is a tough one. On that day, mercy is veiled, and wrath is unveiled; this is a point of no return.

If you look at the sad, poor situation the Muslim world is in today, you would see the points I have raised one by one in this mirror. If you look at the generations who are detached from Allah ❁, the Prophet ❁, the Book of Allah, and at those who lead them in the wrong paths; if you look at those whose souls and hearts have been uprooted and who turned into creatures consisting of the stomach and the intestines; if you look at the headless masses, the thoughtless, irrational, and heedless crowds; if you look at the time that has been lost in vain; and if you look at the history that has been rendered incomprehensible by its broken links, you will see where a huge society has been pushed and you will shudder.

This glorious but unfortunate group of nations, now ruled by the rabble, is writhing and desperate in the clutches of the wicked. The reason why supplications made in the Ka'ba and why tears shed in mosques are fruitless is that they are not the atonement of the sin committed. The way out from a place is the way in at the same time. We have been subjected to this plight for having abandoned a holy duty; we will be saved from this state by fulfilling it. In other words, the most effective supplication to be saved from this state or situation is performing the duty. As such, prayers in tongues alone are not enough for such a plight. Of course, those prayers are useful in the Hereafter. However, the way to get rid of worldly misery is performing the duty of "calling to good and preventing wrong" properly.

As I mentioned in the beginning, a community might have very virtuous people in it. Those people might also be very close to Allah ﷻ in their spiritual aspects. However, if the duty of "calling to good and preventing wrong" is not fulfilled there, if relevant institutions are not established or supported for this purpose, and if this duty is not carried out in a systematic way, Allah ﷻ will turn that community upside down and that community or nation can never be stable and everlasting.

Allah Almighty ﷻ would not punish the entire society because of the sins of a group. He would not hold the entire society accountable for the crimes of a depraved, graceless group of felons or *mutrafin*. *Mutrafin* are those enjoying excessive luxury with no concern for anyone else except themselves. However, if a group of sincere believers who witness *munkarat* (evil acts) do not perform "calling to good and preventing wrong" even though they are able to do so, the punishment will come collectively, to everybody. Let us remember the hadith given above: *"By the One in Whose hand is my soul, you must call to good and prevent wrong, or else Allah will soon send [a common] punishment upon you all. Then, you will call upon Allah and it will not be answered for you."*[36]

The following verse in the Qur'an points to the same possible consequence:

وَاتَّقُوا فِتْنَةً لَا تُصِيبَنَّ الَّذِينَ ظَلَمُوا مِنْكُمْ خَاصَّةً وَاعْلَمُوا اَنَّ اللّٰهَ شَدِيدُ الْعِقَابِ

And beware and guard yourselves against a trial that will not bring punishment only to those among you who are engaged in wrongdoing; and know that Allah is severe in retribution (al-Anfal 8:25).

1.8. Stories of heavenly destructions

We read in history books and holy scriptures the stories of peoples and nations collectively destroyed. It is possible to look into these stories and the destruction of these nations from the perspective of "calling to good and preventing wrong." The fate of a nation is dependent on whether they fulfill this duty or not. If they do, Allah ﷻ does not destroy that group or community. Even if it is a small number of people in that community who perform this holy duty, and if they are not in a position to be overwhelmed and give up their efforts, Allah ﷻ will not destroy that community.

If the duty of "calling to good and preventing wrong" is not done at all by anybody, Allah ﷻ destroys that community with its due punishment. In another scenario, there may be a good number of heroic individuals trying to fulfill this duty, but they are overpowered by the excessive transgressions of others in the community, and eventually they declare they are defeated, and Allah ﷻ destroys that community, too. I will try to explain some aspects of the matter in light of Qur'anic verses. I must state briefly from the very outset that the most effective lightning rod to prevent a nation from being destroyed is its believers' performing this duty with homes and centers of learning they establish. A nation can avoid such a formidable vortex and great turmoil only by serious efforts like these. Now I would like to give a few examples below to illustrate the issue.

a) Prophet Nuh (Noah)

Nuh (peace be upon him) ceaselessly conveyed the Divine Message and tried to spread the Truth throughout his life for almost a thousand years. However, except for a handful individuals, his people reacted to him with denial and persecuted him. It came to a point that Nuh had to open his hands to Almighty Allah ﷻ and confessed that he had been defeated; he prayed for help against the unbelievers. The prayer of such a Prophet was, of course, unrefusable. The Qur'an tells us about this incident in detail:

كَذَّبَتْ قَبْلَهُمْ قَوْمُ نُوحٍ فَكَذَّبُوا عَبْدَنَا وَقَالُوا مَجْنُونٌ وَازْدُجِرَ فَدَعَا رَبَّهُ اَنِّي مَغْلُوبٌ
فَانْتَصِرْ فَفَتَحْنَا اَبْوَابَ السَّمَاءِ بِمَاءٍ مُنْهَمِرٍ وَفَجَّرْنَا الْاَرْضَ عُيُونًا فَالْتَقَى الْمَاءُ عَلٰى
اَمْرٍ قَدْ قُدِرَ وَحَمَلْنَاهُ عَلٰى ذَاتِ اَلْوَاحٍ وَدُسُرٍ تَجْرِي بِاَعْيُنِنَا جَزَاءً لِمَنْ كَانَ كُفِرَ وَلَقَدْ
تَرَكْنَاهَا اٰيَةً فَهَلْ مِنْ مُدَّكِرٍ فَكَيْفَ كَانَ عَذَابِي وَنُذُرِ

Before them (the polytheists who denied Prophet Muhammad ﷺ), the people of Nuh denied: they denied Our servant, and said: "This is a madman!" and he was rebuked (with insolence and prevented from preaching). So he prayed to his Lord, saying: "I have been overcome, so help me!" So We opened the gates of the sky, with water outpouring; And We caused the earth to gush forth with springs, so the waters (of the sky and the earth) combined for (the fulfillment of) a matter already ordained. And We carried him on a (construction of) wooden planks and nails, running (through the water) under Our Eyes as a reward for one who had (wrongfully) been rejected with ingratitude. And indeed We left it (the Ark) as a sign (of the truth). Then is there any that remembers and takes heed? But see how (severe) was My punishment and (how true) My warnings! (Qamar 54:9-16)

Nuh was honored with the gift of Prophethood, a Divine Book, and new law. He was the servant of nobody but Allah ﷻ. He was inviting people to worship only Allah ﷻ and to live good and pure lives. However, his people called him mad, which was in fact a proof of the perfection of his faith. In such a society where the balances of social life were turned upside down and all measures of value were reversed, a Prophet like Nuh would certainly not be considered normal or balanced. Nuh was trying to restore the entire society, which they had ruined. And such a person would, of course, be stigmatized. That is why Prophet Muhammad ﷺ stated in one of his hadiths that should a believer be called a *majnun*, or mad, this would be a point of perfection of his or her faith.[37]

"Help me," prayed Nuh to Allah ﷻ. "I am overwhelmed, help me!" Upon hearing this prayer, Allah ﷻ submerged his raging people with the waters coming from above and below. Maybe it was the Atlantean civilization, maybe not; maybe it was the Atlantic Ocean or another sea… Such details do not matter. What matters is that a civilization was sinking despite the fact that there was a Prophet among them, and he was trying to call them to good and prevent wrong, and yet that Prophet declared himself defeated. After giving the full account of the event, the verse asks: "Then is there any that remembers and takes heed?"

By the way, let me make my addition here and ask, "Is there any of my fellow citizens that will receive admonition from the ruins of Sardis?[8] Isn't there anyone who will take an example from the ruins of Pergamon[9] and cry? Is there any that will receive admonition from Troy[10]? Is there any that will receive admonition from all these and similar sites?" Hundreds of ruins on earth, each of them is the evidence of sinful communities and nations perished. They are all evidence or witnesses before our eyes. Is there indeed any that will heed warnings and receive admonition?

b) Prophet Salih

Prophet Salih's[11] (pbuh) people, the Thamud, grew heedless and disobeyed him. As Salih continued to urge his people to believe, Allah ﷻ supported him with a miraculous she-camel. Salih told them to leave her alone and warned them of possible destruction if they did not. Unfortunately, they could not restrain themselves from the temptation and slaughtered the miraculous camel.

"Not touching a camel" may strain some people's understanding at

8 Sardis was the capital of the ancient Kingdom of Lydia, ruled by King Croesus (560-546 BC), in the Central Aegean Region of Türkiye.

9 Pergamon (also Pergamum) was a major intellectual and cultural center in Mysiain, modern-day Türkiye, which flourished as the capital of the Kingdom of Pergamon under the Attalid Dynasty (281-133 BCE).

10 Troy is the name of the large and prosperous Bronze Age city occupied over millennia and attacked in the Trojan War, a popular story in the mythology of ancient Greece, in the north-west of Türkiye.

11 Sometimes written as Saleh in English. Prophet Salih was a descendant of Nuh and Allah ﷻ sent him to the nation of Thamud who lived in Al-Hijr, located in Arabia. The nation was proud, and disobedient to warnings. They were leading an affluent life in their huge castles, palaces, and other structures that were carved out of sheer rock, which were the manifestation of all their power, materialism, and arrogance.

first. People may not see the wisdom in it immediately. However, human beings have always been under obligations in every age. Prayer, fasting, alms are some of these obligations. Similarly, it is also an obligation not to consume intoxicants, not to commit adultery, and not to charge usury. These or many similar obligations may vary and can sometimes be in the form of, as in the case of the Thamud, "not touching a camel," which they failed to observe. The chapter *ash-Shams* (the Sun) in the Qur'an reveals this incident to us as follows:

كَذَّبَتْ ثَمُودُ بِطَغْوٰيهَاۤ اِذِ انْبَعَثَ اَشْقٰيهَاۖ فَقَالَ لَهُمْ رَسُولُ اللّٰهِ نَاقَةَ اللّٰهِ وَسُقْيٰيهَاۜ فَكَذَّبُوهُ فَعَقَرُوهَاۙ فَدَمْدَمَ عَلَيْهِمْ رَبُّهُمْ بِذَنْبِهِمْ فَسَوّٰيهَاۙ

The (tribe of) Thamud denied (the Divine Message and their Messenger, and displayed their denial) in their arrogant rebellion. (Especially) when (finally) the most wicked among them (instigated by his people) rushed forward. The Messenger of Allah (Salih) said: "It is the she-camel of Allah, and observe her turn in drinking." But they denied him and slaughtered her; and so their Lord crushed them for their sin, and leveled them (with the ground). (ash-Shams 91:11-14)

In the face of this arrogant rebellion, Prophet Salih was in a position only to counsel them verbally. He warned them not to touch her, because it would be, as it were, touching the button of trouble. But his people did not listen to him, and someone who was at the forefront of rebellion, and who of course represented other disobedient ones, touched this button of a heavenly calamity.

This has always been the case in all periods. Someone leading in unbelief appears and others follow him en masse. Some attacked religion or the Qur'an, for instance, and by doing so they triggered the collapse of an entire nation. Later, the personalities would change, but the scenario would continue. Those who would defile the Ka'ba and pollute the *Zamzam* (water from the holy well of *zamzam)* have always existed and will exist in every age.

When a wicked person stepped forward to slaughter the camel, the Thamud remained silent to it and prepared their own fate. Allah ﷻ levelled them collectively, both those who perpetrated the crime and those who did not intervene. The Thamud, now buried in the tomb of the past, were not only subjected to physical destruction, but their good name was also brought into disrepute.

Sometimes calamity does not come to the body; disfiguration or deformation (*maskh*) may happen not in the appearance or physical image but in the inner, moral qualities of a person or a community. In fact, such a scourge is more difficult to realize and more severe than the calamity that hits only the physical body. The disasters that come today seem to be mainly of this kind. I think that's one reason why the disobedience or arrogant defiance continues to be dizzyingly arbitrary, for people are not aware of the real trouble that is swirling above their heads. The chapter ends with *"And for Him is no fear of its consequences"* (ash-Shams 91:15 وَلَا يَخَافُ عُقْبٰيهَا), pointing to the fact that Allah ﷻ is the Lord of the whole creation, everything is at His disposal; thus, He is not the one to fear the consequences of any calamity.

In the light of the verses of the chapter ash-Shams, we see that during the turmoil, in which the Prophet Salih was about to fall defeated and was unable to make his people listen to his advice and obey Allah ﷻ, Allah ﷻ annihilated those people. The creation of the universe, and especially the human being, is for a particular reason: that Allah ﷻ is known and worshipped. When believers are defeated—that is, when conveying the message and spiritual guidance cannot be fulfilled or such efforts do not produce any result—creation is left without a reason to exist. Then Allah Almighty ﷻ shakes the people of that era, and sometimes, as in the examples above, He destroys them. This is a Divine law that never changes and will never change.

c) Prophet Lut

Prophet Lut (Lot) was a contemporary of Prophet Ibrahim, and he was sent as a Prophet to invite to faith the wicked people of Sodom and Gomorrah, located on the border of Jordan and Palestine. These were a people who would waylay travelers and commit indecent activities in their gatherings. But the most notorious act of evil that was committed by this corrupt nation was open and widespread sodomy. Prophet Lut started to inform people of the error of their ways and invited them to enter into the path of Allah ﷻ. He said:

إِنَّكُمْ لَتَأْتُونَ الرِّجَالَ شَهْوَةً مِنْ دُونِ النِّسَاءِ بَلْ أَنْتُمْ قَوْمٌ مُسْرِفُونَ

"You come to men with lust in place of women. You are a people committing excesses and wasteful (of your Allah-given faculties)" (al-A'raf 7:81)

The people of Sodom became very disgruntled at Lut's mission and planned to drive him out from their city. So, Prophet Lut prayed: *"My Lord, support me against the corrupting people. My Lord, save me and my family from what they do."*

Answering his prayers, Allah ﷻ sent three angels to Prophet Lut disguised as handsome young men. But the word quickly spread in the town, and the mobs immediately gathered at Lut's doorstep, demanding these young men. Lut responded almost in a manner of begging: "Have fear of Allah, and do not disgrace me in respect of my guests. Is there not among you one right-minded man?" In an effort to give them a lawful option, he suggested marrying off his daughters, but to no avail. They said:

قَالُوا لَقَدْ عَلِمْتَ مَا لَنَا فِي بَنَاتِكَ مِنْ حَقٍّ وَاِنَّكَ لَتَعْلَمُ مَا نُرِيدُ

"You know well that we have no claim on your daughters; and you surely know well what we desire" (Hud 11:79)

Prophet Lut became helpless against the corrupt people, sighed deeply, and said:

قَالَ لَوْ اَنَّ لِي بِكُمْ قُوَّةً اَوْ اٰوِي اِلٰى رُكْنٍ شَدِيدٍ

"O! Would that I had power to resist you, or that I could lean upon some strong support!" (Hud 11:80). He had a strong foothold and support, but these words show how desperate he felt under that difficult situation. Lut breathed a sigh of relief when the angels revealed their true identity and said:

قَالُوا يَا لُوطُ اِنَّا رُسُلُ رَبِّكَ لَنْ يَصِلُوا اِلَيْكَ

"O Lut! We are envoys of your Lord. They will not reach you" (Hud 11:81). The angels continued:

فَاَسْرِ بِاَهْلِكَ بِقِطْعٍ مِنَ الَّيْلِ وَلَا يَلْتَفِتْ مِنْكُمْ اَحَدٌ اِلَّا امْرَاَتَكَ اِنَّهُ مُصِيبُهَا مَا اَصَابَهُمْ اِنَّ مَوْعِدَهُمُ الصُّبْحُ اَلَيْسَ الصُّبْحُ بِقَرِيبٍ فَلَمَّا جَاءَ اَمْرُنَا جَعَلْنَا عَالِيَهَا سَافِلَهَا وَاَمْطَرْنَا عَلَيْهَا حِجَارَةً مِنْ سِجِّيلٍ مَنْضُودٍ مُسَوَّمَةً عِنْدَ رَبِّكَ وَمَا هِيَ مِنَ الظَّالِمِينَ بِبَعِيدٍ

"So, set out with your family in a part of the night, and let no one among you turn round all save your wife, for that which is to befall them will befall her as well. Their appointed time is the morning. Is the morning not near?"

So when Our judgment came to pass, We overturned (those sinful towns), and rained down on them stones of baked clay one after another. (Each stone) marked out by your Lord (for a particular individual).

And they are never far from wrongdoers (in all times and places). (Hud 11:81-83)

Sodom and Gomorrah perished and was submerged deep in the Dead Sea. However, this punishment was not reserved only for the people of Lut. The oppressors of every era would suffer the same fate. Here is Pompeii, the most striking example of this. There were Christians who were spreading truth there, but they too were defeated. The nation was in such debauchery and misery that they were already dead in spirit when Allah ﷻ turned the city into a cemetery with the lava gushing from Vesuvius. Although some of them had fled to the seashore, piles of ashes as big as houses came and buried them there as well.

Allah ﷻ rendered each of those places, in a sense, a museum of signs and evidence so that future generations draw a moral lesson and that everyone can read accordingly the outcome of their deeds there. Today on the walls that remain from Pompeii, it is possible to see the most disgusting obscenity which proves their excessive indulgence and rampant debauchery. Yes, the Almighty has left them like an exemplary warning sign so the wise ones can see and draw a moral from them.

d) And others...

Allah Almighty ﷻ has seized and punished people who defiantly rejected His Message and Prophets in the past. This is His universal law, and it is not peculiar to one nation or time-period. With this law, He has executed His Divine Will and Judgment in the same way over other nations throughout history.

For example, Andalusian civilization was one magnificent civilization and lasted for eight centuries. Muslims who first arrived in Spain and Portugal to establish Andalusia with dignity had to leave it in disgrace by Ferdinand's sword when they lost their virtuous attributes. Their defeat was embarrassing and took place in tears. However, the time to cry was long gone. Besides, when they were crying, they were not crying for the right thing. It was necessary and would be enough for them to weep as to why they had to build lavish baths in Toledo. They had to weep at the fact that they had destroyed their raison d'être with their own hands. Alas, they were crying instead only for their own funerals.

It was this misery of the soul that destroyed the Abbasids, too. The same kind of dirty things and degeneration destroyed the Umayyad. The Seljuks experienced the bitter fate of living lightheaded at the collapse of their Empire. The fate of the Ottomans was the result of the same spiritual decadence. When you enter Dolmabahçe Palace in Istanbul, when you hear that sixteen tons of gold was spent only on gilding at a time when the entire country was in regression, you will shudder and see with your own eyes the destruction of the Ottomans on the walls of the palace. This is a Divine law, and it has never changed—and will never change.

You may consider all historical ethnographic museums—from the fall of Rome to the fall of the Sassanids, and from there to the fall of Egypt—based on this rule. Allah ﷻ destroys a community or a land where His Message is not taught or conveyed. Because that place is no longer what it was created for in the first place. I assume that this will be the reason for the end of the world. When believers are completely weakened and overcome, and the disbelief becomes as wide and fierce as possible, Allah ﷻ will turn the whole world upside down. That is to say that the world does not sustain the purpose of its existence.

When the Qur'an becomes a book whose message is not understood, one should know that an encroaching shadow of troubles and calamities is upon us. If the destruction is not coming, it is thanks to Allah's ﷻ boundless mercy. Caliph Abu Bakr would sometimes be overwhelmed and enraptured by the All-Encompassing Mercy of Allah ﷻ and say, "How clement you are my Lord."[38] Indeed He is clement, He gives the sinners respite and delays their penalty for a while, but once He seizes, they are done for.[39] We must think of the fact that Allah ﷻ introduces Himself to us as the All-Compassionate and the All-Merciful. Since He is indeed so, it is incumbent upon us to know Him as such and to respond to this mercy by being a proper and sincere servant to Him, especially by being a trustworthy spiritual guide who leads people's hearts to Allah ﷻ with the promise of faith and security.

In fact, a true believer is first and foremost a person of security. No harm should be expected from them. Believers are like an insurance policy for all humanity and for a safe society. Believers may feel a bit more affable towards other believers, but they are in a position to share with everyone the beauties and goodness they have received from Allah

ﷻ and His Messenger ﷺ. They should act very sincerely and sensitively as they try to restore the society on the one hand and protect it from various harms on the other. Those who do not want to undertake this duty are, in a sense, renouncing the title of "believer" given to them as a sign of honor.

From the smallest circle—which is the circle of one's heart and soul—to the largest circle, which include one's household, neighborhood, town, city, country, and humanity as a whole, believers have duties and obligations according to their own status and position. If people in all those circles are to reach a bright future, that will be by the enlightening words and deeds of believers. The negligence of believers at fulfilling these duties and obligations is a big responsibility, for it will cause a major deprivation of other people, even if those people are not aware of it.

If disbelief is not addressed properly, not only disbelievers but also believers will suffer and lose. Therefore, at least, from this point of view, too, the believer should fulfil the duty of "calling to good and preventing wrong" not to give way to a collective disaster. Concerning this point, Allah's Messenger ﷺ said:

"The example of the person abiding by Allah's order and restrictions in comparison to those who violate them is like the example of those persons who drew lots for their seats in a boat. Some of them got seats in the upper part, and the others in the lower. When the latter needed water, they had to go up to bring water (and that troubled the others), so they said, 'Let us make a hole in our share of the ship (and get water) saving those who are above us from troubling them.' So, if the people in the upper part let the others do what they had suggested, all the people of the ship would be destroyed, but if they prevented them, both parties would be safe."[40]

The desire of those who want to dig a hole in the boat, at first glance, may seem innocent. However, what this will result in is not innocent at all. With this analogy, the Prophet explains the possible consequences of a serious societal problem.

Based on this hadith, it can be said that the world is a boat, like Nuh's ark. All of humanity has boarded this boat without any choice, for this is the only place all humanity can live. In other words, the boat we live on and travel with is the only one, and there is no second boat. The order of life on this boat belongs to the One Who put us here. Others shall have no right to violate this order. And under these circumstances, there is no specific life to be excluded.

It is the duty of all of us to protect our boat from sinking. This duty is an obligation that is placed on our shoulders as we board the boat. We do not have the luxury to be too "humane" not to interfere in other people's business and allow them to damage the boat, putting everyone's life at risk.

Therefore, on the one hand, we are obliged to tackle and remove *munkarat* (all kinds of evil and wickedness) in the community, and thus to protect humanity from their harm and damage. On the other hand, we have to equip and furnish community with *ma'ruf* (all the good deeds and virtuous behaviors). In fact, the community formed by sound characters and impeccable natures would also be free from all kinds of evil. This, however, is one aspect of the matter; the other aspect is to work hard to ensure benevolent things flourish in the community. This is heavy and difficult, but it is a sacred duty.

A believer, once he or she tastes the joy of true belief, invites others to get their share from that joy—they do this out of their *muruwwah*: generosity, wisdom, and benevolence. A believer is an embodiment of these virtues. As they feel like they are experiencing springtime, they wish that others should also enjoy and benefit from it, and they strive to make this possible. After all, a true believer is one who devotes his or her life to the happiness of others—they give up their own desires for the joy of living for others.

Once the light of faith enters a heart, how is it possible for that person to stand still and not act? It is this impossibility that makes the believer go from one house to another, from one business to another, and from one store to another, in order to find familiar hearts. In a sense, fulfilling this duty is an insurance policy of a believer's own existence. A policy to assure preserving faith for a lifetime and to pass away with that commitment. Not performing the duty of "calling to good and preventing wrong" risks losing this policy. This is why believers must perform this sacred duty at least in order to save themselves.

1.9. A measure of preserving religion

The religion of Islam is under Allah's ﷻ protection. There is a Divine promise Islam will maintain its original purity until the Day of Judgment. However, this preservation only happens through the effort of Muslims. In other words, Allah makes Muslims' efforts a basic condition of His protecting Islam. As long as this is the will of Allah ﷻ, and as long as Muslims strive for it, this religion will be protected. Allah's ﷻ promise should rather be perceived this way.

Believers must safeguard the religion. If pious ones do not safeguard and promulgate their religion, they become deprived of its Divine emanations and blessings. This never means that the religion is not, or will not be, protected by Allah ﷻ. That deprivation needs to be understood as follows: maybe believers did not act or not take action when necessary, with their own free will, to safeguard their religion. For human's free choice or will is considered to be a condition for the Will and creation of Allah ﷻ to come into existence. Therefore, Muslims' being made miserable by Allah ﷻ, being deprived of His blessings, and also the decline in religious belief and practice today should be understood as such. The religion will be safeguarded by Allah ﷻ by means of the believers' protection. Likewise, the religion will rise and thrive to the extent its followers convey it to others.

The Messenger of Allah ﷺ did what he could to support the religion and Allah ﷻ protected His religion. For centuries, Muslims did what they could to support the religion, and again Allah ﷻ safeguarded it. When the support given to the religion loosened, Allah ﷻ made people distraught or devastated. The Messenger of Allah ﷺ treated this subject as the most important issue. Day and night he tried to warn his *ummah*, his community of believers, on this matter. Happiness in the Hereafter depends on one's observing his or her faith in this world. Eventually, the only way of giving a good account of oneself on the Judgment Day, crossing the heavenly bridge (*al-sirat*) quickly to enter Paradise, and seeing the Lord Almighty, is serving faith, performing good and righteous deeds, and having a pure, sound heart.

The Messenger of Allah ﷺ strove continuously to be able to give such a passport to his *ummah*. Spreading the message to others was the principal issue for him. His efforts and diligence aroused the same consciousness among his community. They, too, sincerely embraced and supported the religion. These efforts were never in vain. Allah ﷻ responded to their efforts by protecting religion and rewarded them in the best way. The Companions were almost competing with one another to convey the messages they received from the Messenger to the four corners of the world. What they knew in the name of religion was perhaps five or ten verses, five or ten hadiths, but they were both living what they knew and trying to spread it to the world.

The reason why the Companion Mus'ab ibn Umayr went from Mecca to Medina was to realize this purpose, to convey the message. He went all alone to this very faraway town. There was no one accompanying him. When some time before the people of Medina had come to the Prophet and asked for a teacher to teach them the religion, the Prophet ﷺ assigned Mus'ab ibn Umayr to do it. In Medina, Mus'ab was staying as a guest in a house. Everyday a few people from the notables of Medina came to him, and he told them about the religion. Usayd ibn Hudayr, Sa'd ibn Ubada, and Sa'd ibn Mu'adh were among those who came to listen to Mus'ab.[41]

Those who came with swords in their hands were returning with faith in their hearts. Mus'ab treated the great companions of the future with such remarkable modesty and decorum that even the harshest man could not long resist his gentle behavior. "My friend, listen to me first, and then take my head off if you want. I'm not going to retaliate against you," Mus'ab said to his visitors. Such an encounter with a person whose biggest concern or purpose was only to tell people the truth was slowly melting the ice, and the circle of people around Mus'ab expanded with each passing day. Until the battle of Badr, Mus'ab spent his life disseminating the Message to others. Then was a time to spread the call, and the duty of the Companions on that day was to convey the Message and guide people to the Truth.[42]

Conveying the Message is an obligation, while protecting it is another. At the battle of Uhud, the Companions had to defend and protect their faith and community against the polytheist onslaught. Mus'ab was also among those heroes of protection. He fought in such a way that even the angels envied him. At one point, Mus'ab was hit with a fatal blow, and he fell face down. The story goes that immediately an angel disguised himself as Mus'ab and continued his fight. Towards the end of the battle, when the Messenger of Allah ﷺ called out to him, the angel said, "I am not Mus'ab, O Allah's Messenger!" Then it was discovered that Mus'ab had already been martyred.[43]

Later the Messenger of Allah ﷺ and a group of Companions found Mus'ab's fallen body. Both of his arms were cut off at the shoulder. Another blow almost tore his head off. Yet, Mus'ab looked as if he was hiding his face from something. The rest of the story is told in a weak narration as follows:

Only the Messenger of Allah had been able to understand why Mus'ab was hiding his face. He told this to the Companions in tears: "Do you know why Mus'ab hid his face? The first reason is that his arms were severed and he would no longer be able to protect the Prophet. 'What if someone attacked the Prophet at this time and I could not rush to the Prophet's aid,' he thought. The second reason is that he thought, 'Now I am about to pass away and go to the presence of the Lord Almighty. Yet, I have to protect the Prophet even at this moment. What if they do something to him, how am I going to show my face to Allah?' So, he hid his face."[44] When the Messenger of Allah said this, he was interpreting and voicing the thoughts of a very sincere hero of truth. However, Mus'ab was not alone that day[45]; all the Companions had the same spirit and consciousness. Allah rewarded their magnanimity and sincerity by protecting His religion.

Allah's ﷻ protection of the religion lasted for some time, which was followed by some unfavorable events. Because Muslims did not uphold their faith during such events, Allah ﷻ partly cut off His blessings from them. We can claim our faith only to the extent that we own and protect it. In case we do not, it is inevitable that Allah ﷻ will deprive us of those emanations and favors that would otherwise come by observing our faith.

Salahuddin Al Ayyubi, also known as Saladin in the West, is famously known to have not laughed for years while Jerusalem was under the Crusader occupation. The story goes that one day when he was attending a prayer service in a mosque, the imam spoke about the importance and benefits of smiling. After the prayer, as the imam was passing by, Salahuddin reached out to his hand and said, "I think you alluded to me in your words. But tell me for Allah's ﷻ sake, how can I laugh when the mosque the Prophet ﷺ ascended to the heavens from is in the hands of enemies?" It is also told that Salahuddin refused to live in a proper house, living instead in a tent, saying that he would not live in a house "when the house of Allah ﷻ is a prisoner." This is how they protected their religion, and they could claim Islam for themselves. Now it is our turn to take on this duty which is binding upon each believer. Today, upholding Islam is done by representing it properly and conveying its message. No believer is exempt from this. Every believer should first be well educated about the religion, live it properly, and make it an intrinsic part of their lives, then enlighten others with the Divine light. Islam charges every believer with this duty.

At this point, I would like to underline certain reasons why today's Muslims have fallen into the sad situation they are in. The gradual decline of Muslims' proper care and observance of their faith is the first reason. The second reason is the establishment of a clerical class—as has been the case in some other religious traditions—and leaving religious services exclusively under their official authority. This is at least as dangerous as the first reason. For one thing, religion cannot be monopolized. It can never be made the property of a particular class or a group. Religion belongs to all believers. Every individual has their own attachment and adherence to Allah Almighty ﷻ. Just as it is not possible to eliminate this private adherence of individuals to Allah ﷻ, so, too, is it impossible to prevent them from individually upholding and protecting the religion. In Islam, monopolizing religious services by inventing a clerical organization is heedlessness, an inexcusable mistake. It is not possible for us to get out of the heartbreaking situation we are in until we avoid this heedlessness. Every individual must uphold their religion so that the expected prosperity and salvation can find its way into us. Any act contrary to this is an obstacle preventing the religion from manifesting its own power, which is destined to take place eventually. In fact, putting religious services at the disposal of a particular organization alone has nothing to do with Islam's understanding of religious endeavor and guidance. Islam is not a religion to be confined to the mosque only. It was sent to make both our world and the Hereafter prosperous.

Islam is such a whole that it cannot be divided into parts and sections. One cannot pick-and-choose only those aspects of Islam that are observed in the mosque but not those that are outside the mosque. We will be freed from the misery and disgrace the day we consider and evaluate religion as a whole and internalize it in our souls. Once we can do this, the illuminating rays of the Revelation will resolve our issues both at the individual and collective level and people will be saved from floundering in darkness.

In order to attain such a state, we will first have to turn with all our hearts to Islam, which is based on the Divine Revelation and enlightening statements of the Prophet, and we will then have to enlighten our inner world with that Divine light. I must remind you once again that Allah ﷻ will not change the condition of a people until they change what is in themselves (Ar-Ra'd 13:11). This is the case whether the condition is a positive or a negative one. It is according to the straightforwardness and steadfastness of individuals that Allah ﷻ will maintain your condition. Just as the deviation of individuals takes away religious life, the straightforwardness and steadfastness of the individuals will bring it back and restore it. Therefore, what is essential is informing and educating the individuals one by one and thus letting them uphold and protect their own religion.

We must keep in mind that sound individuals constitute sound families, and sound families constitute sound societies. The individual and then the family are the basis of society. It is never possible to establish a sound society without educating, reforming, and improving them. A sound community is a community that continues to exist within the guidelines determined by Allah ﷻ and His Messenger ﷺ. For this to be possible, it is essential that every heart be equipped with the *ma'ruf* (all the good deeds and virtuous behaviors) and cleansed from the *munkarat* (all kinds of evil and wickedness). Each heart should be equipped with good qualities and cleansed off bad qualities so that the society can continue its existence in this line. It is the individuals who will do this. All the guidelines in this regard have been directly revealed to us by Allah ﷻ and His Messenger ﷺ.

Conveying the message and spiritual guidance that are not carried out within these guidelines can never produce the desired result. Allah ﷻ does not give His consent to, or approve of, the way we go if it is other than the way He willed and prescribed. Even if all the world approves but Allah ﷻ does not, it is to no avail. The more we are with Allah ﷻ, the more His Grace and Mercy are with us.

Our ill fortune will be changed only by the blessed ones who uphold the religion and maintain their attachment to Divine Grace and Mercy consistently. Let me emphasize once again we can claim our faith to the extent that we uphold and safeguard it.

Chapter 2

Guidelines

Every scientific discipline has a particular definition. Every business requires following a certain procedure. One can hardly talk about a scientific discipline or business without reference to such definitions and procedures. Likewise, one naturally assumes the necessity of following a set of guidelines when one engages in spiritual guidance, which is the most esteemed, honored, and blessed duty. A duty done without complying with and respecting its working principles will be of no more use than a pitiful zeal. Certain accomplishments mean an implicit failure or defeat because they are temporary and do not promise a sustainable future.

In this chapter, I intend to present some technical principles with regards to the duty of conveying the Message. What you will find in the coming pages does not constitute the only methodology for teaching about Islam. However, as a person who has spent his life among the scholars, spiritual masters, and preachers, and as someone who has assumed this duty in various capacities for most of his life, I have tried to compile these guidelines in the light of the Qur'anic verses and Prophetic traditions in a way that hopefully allows them to be implemented in real life. Among my expressions, imperfections that are irreconcilable with the reality of the world or life must be regarded as the products of my own shortcomings. The thoughts and ideas that are entitled to live on are those that are not only talked but also walked. This has been a maxim for me as well.

2.1. Knowledge

It is essential that those who will "call to good and prevent wrong" are equipped with knowledge. For knowledge and conveying the message are like two faces of the same truth. A spiritual guide must educate himself or herself very well in terms of religion before they start teaching others. Otherwise, they may make serious mistakes in the name of religion and scare away others both from themselves and the religion. Such a consequence is, in a sense, depriving people of what they deserve, the implications of which concern both this world and the next.

In this chapter, I will discuss and explain first our understanding of knowledge and then the relationship between conveying the message, knowledge, and practicing one's faith (deeds, action).

With respect to the whole creation, knowledge is like the direction of prayer, *qiblah*, just as Prophet Adam was to angels.[12] Knowledge becomes an engineering marvel in the form of a ship with Prophet Nuh; in the Ark, knowledge takes the form of Nuh himself.

Knowledge expands as large as valleys in the case of Prophet Ibrahim—valleys that receive a torrential downpour of Divine Revelation. Knowledge becomes Mount Sinai with Prophet Musa or Musa himself on Mount Sinai. Everything in the universe is, as it were, a mold, or a vessel. Yet, the essence of the universe is knowledge.

What is knowledge then? What kind of knowledge reveals, manifests and informs us of the true essence of things and beings? What is its relation with the Almighty Creator?

Knowledge is knowing one's Lord, the Creator, through the lenses of knowing one's self, the created. One seeing his or her Lord by observing themself or contemplating Allah's ﷻ Attributes and Names with what they discovered in their perceptions and feelings...This is the real knowledge.

The famous poet Yunus Emre underscores the ultimate purpose or outcome of knowledge to be studying and learning:

Knowledge is to know
To know your self
If you do not know your self
How is this learning?

12 "Allah taught Adam the names, all of them" (al-Baqarah 2:31). This verse points to the knowledge taught to Prophet Adam, peace be upon him, signifying the supremacy of humankind, for later in 2:34 angels are commanded to "prostrate before Adam" as if he was in the directon of prayer, *qiblah*.

"The one who knows oneself knows Allah ﷻ"[46] is a wise statement, and people often mistake it for a hadith, although it is not. Supporting this meaning, the Qur'an says:

وَلَا تَكُونُوا كَالَّذِينَ نَسُوا اللهَ فَأَنْسٰيهُمْ أَنْفُسَهُمْ أُولٰٓئِكَ هُمُ الْفَاسِقُونَ

And do not be like those who are oblivious of Allah and so Allah has made them oblivious of their own selves. Those, they are the transgressors. (al-Hashr 59:19)

If you forget Allah ﷻ, He makes you forget your own self, your soul. When you forget your soul, you turn away and move further apart from Allah ﷻ. Thus, a vicious circle forms, causing further detrimental concentric circles of forgetting. Whoever enters such a vicious circle can hardly escape from it, and they eventually perish.

The following meaning can also be inferred from the verse: Do not ever forget Allah ﷻ; otherwise, He makes you forget your self. Then you would start to be interested and engaged with the world outside of you. Your sight or perspectives would always focus on external, worldly matters. You would never turn your contemplative perspectives on your self and not hold it to account. You say "Islam"; however, you seek it in others' lives. You say "the Qur'an"; but you expect others, rather than yourself, to live by the Qur'anic wisdom. While those closest to you in your home are flagrantly violating Islamic precepts, you ignore them and always center your interests and expectations on others. How sad it is to march in the streets cheering for Islam, but in fact walking behind the devil while doing so!

In order not to fall into such a situation, we must first make a very good self-accounting and review our relationship with the Lord several times a day. Just like mountaineers, we have to be alert and attentive not to make the slightest mistake. We have to check properly every crack where we place our hands and feet. We have to place wedges and nuts and other forms of protection into the rocks, so that we may not slip and fall, for the slightest mistake we make can cost us our lives.

Forgetting oneself is worst when one is in a place of worship, for those are the places where believers have to be very alert, conscious, inward looking, and self-reckoning. Unfortunately, there are many who forget themselves even in places as holy as the Ka'ba in Mecca and the Prophet's mosque in Medina. What a loss it is! What a pity it is!

Knowledge has a purpose: to guide a believer to knowledge of Allah ﷻ (*ma'rifah*) and His love (*mahabbah*). The knowledge that does not ignite the love of Allah ﷻ in the heart and does not inflame one's spiritual contentment that promises the blessings of Paradise cannot be considered to have achieved its goal. The knowledge that has achieved its purpose is the source of life to our innermost subtleties and finer faculties. It is the lifeblood of our senses. Its deprivation is a spiritual death. In fact, the knowledge that the Qur'an and the hadiths exalt and encourage is none other than this.

قُلْ هَلْ يَسْتَوِي الَّذِينَ يَعْلَمُونَ وَالَّذِينَ لَا يَعْلَمُونَ إِنَّمَا يَتَذَكَّرُ أُولُوا الْأَلْبَابِ

Say: "Are they ever equal, those who know and those who do not know?" Only the people of discernment will reflect (on the distinction between knowledge and ignorance, and obedience to Allah and disobedience,) and be mindful. (az-Zumar 39:9)

Consider two kinds of knowledge. On the one hand, the knowledge that takes a person by the hand and leads them to Allah ﷻ; and on the other, the knowledge that enslaves another person with hard labor in the laboratory but leads nowhere? One type of knowledge makes a person look through the telescope with the right perspective and intention and has them observe nothing but a heavenly stairway to Allah ﷻ; while another type of knowledge fixates another person's eyes on the visible aspects of stars and celestial systems, but not beyond: can these two be equal? Or rather, are these two different viewholders ever considered equal? On the one hand, the so-called scientist or scholar who wanders among the books like a cellar mouse and who spends their lifetime writing annotations, references, and commentaries, but who does not read a single line of the knowledge of truth—or rather, who, in the words of the Qur'an, like a donkey that carries, transports what it does not understand.[47] On the other hand, the true human being, who hovers into the heavenly skies with a single sentence they read and who thus feels another instant of the attainment of Divine Blessings each moment? Are these two groups of people equal now?

I think there is as much difference between them as there is between "nothing" and "everything." The knowledge that leads to Allah ﷻ is "everything"; the knowledge that leaves one abandoned is "nothing."

إِنَّمَا يَخْشَى اللّٰهَ مِنْ عِبَادِهِ الْعُلَمٰٓؤُا

Of all of Allah's servants, only the knowledgeable are truly in awe of Him. (Fatir 35:28)

As obvious as it is, knowledge and the learned are praised in this verse. But this glorification is in the case of the person who reveres the Lord with his or her knowledge. Every knowledge has its own weight and status. The Messenger of Allah ﷺ states that the true scholars are the true heirs of the Prophets.[48]

If there is a group on earth that can perceive the absolute truth without any loss, it is the Prophets. We, on the other hand, have the opportunity to penetrate the inner face of the truths only through the beams of light that the Prophets impart to us. It is impossible for a person to find the absolute truth without the tutelage of a Prophet. Perhaps one can discover certain truths with their own efforts and diligence. But the "absolute truth" can be discovered only with the spiritual guidance of the Prophets. Consequently, the true heirs of Allah ﷻ on earth are the Prophets and after them the righteous servants of Allah ﷻ. The Qur'an points to the righteous servants as the heirs to the earth,[49] which shows an obvious connection between the expression of our Prophet and the meaning expressed by this verse. In other words, righteous servants who deserve to inherit the earth are the learned ones who are heir to the Prophets. The Prophet is the interpreter of the truth, so any human being is heir to the Prophet to the extent he or she interprets and conveys the truth.

The Messenger of Allah ﷺ makes the following comparison to show the distinguished status of a true scholar:

"The superiority of the learned man over the worshiper is like my superiority over the least of you."[50]

A person can be a devout worshipper. But if he or she is not a learned person, it is quite possible that they may not maintain their stability in faith and slip away. This slip is relative to everyone's status in the sight of Allah ﷻ. There are such people that even if they fail to contemplate Allah ﷻ and forget His Grace for even a moment, this is considered to be a serious deviation. More precisely, it is a deviation in the eyes of that person. In the case of the learned person who is heir to the Prophet ﷺ, he or she is in continuous contemplation, self-control, and self-accounting. They are always vigilant and maintain continuous metaphysical consciousness of dangers. The learned person who performs their acts of worship with awareness and deals with every issue in a conscious way is superior to the one who worships but is not mindful of it, just as our Prophet ﷺ was superior to his Companions. In fact, this means that there is no comparison between the two.

Another aspect of this issue is that the righteous person who is the heir of the Prophet does not miss any ray of light that comes from the Prophet. Like a big power plant absorbing radiation coming from the sun, the righteous person makes their heart active with all its faculties. They try to receive all blessings coming from Him, without missing a single particle, as the manifestation of His Oneness, Grace, Beauty, and Infinite Mercy. They try to reflect the Divine emanations bestowed upon them in its entirety.

This is also the expression of their respect towards their Lord and a process of charging themselves spiritually. Whoever continuously charges in this way discharges and transmits the lights and truths within their soul onto others. And their inner motivation is so grand that the value it brings to what they do cannot be measured against any scale. Therefore, no matter how deep an ordinary believer deepens in their worship, they can hardly perform a worship equivalent to the deeds of the learned, righteous, true human being (*al-insan al-kamil*). Moreover, a person must absolutely act according to their knowledge. The Qur'an warns those who fail do to so as follows:

فَرِيقًا مِنْهُمْ لَيَكْتُمُونَ الْحَقَّ وَهُمْ يَعْلَمُونَ

There is a group of them who, even though they know it, conceal the truth. (al-Baqarah 2:146)

They know but they do not act accordingly. They are almost like black holes in space. They take in much but get out or give almost nothing. No one can make use of the potential of light such people possess. In other words, they cannot be like the sun. The sun functions like a fireplace to warm, a lamp to illuminate, and a spectrum of colors to beautify our world. The sun caresses the heads of the flowers in our planet; at the same time, it sends beams of light to all the planets which are like the sun's flowers. Let us not spend more time on the unfortunate people who entrap the empowering light with their own darkness despite their enormous potential, and now move onto another hadith of the Prophet as a matter of interest:

"Whoever is asked about some knowledge that he knows, then he conceals it, he will be bridled on the Day of Resurrection with reins of fire."[51]

The meaning of this blessed word is also clear. Whoever learns something good and then does not share it with others, who does not disseminate it around, who does not set a good example with his words and deeds, who does not represent the truth and reflect it around—that is, who does not discharge the benevolent gains—the punishment for this crime is to curb his mouth with a bridle of fire in the Hereafter. This is quite a serious admonition, for only animals are bridled. The person who conceals his knowledge fails to appreciate many things: the fact that Allah ﷻ created him or her in the most excellent pattern; the gift of being able to express their feelings and thoughts; and the faculty or virtue of reasoning placed in their nature, which distinguishes them from animals. By concealing knowledge and not conveying it to the others, they certainly do not thank Allah ﷻ in return for these faculties and virtues. As a just treatment in the Hereafter, Allah ﷻ then takes back those blessings from the person who concealed and misused them in this world.

Knowledge and conveying the message along with spiritual guidance are two aspects of the same truth. As to putting into practice one's knowledge, or acting upon it accordingly, it is the indispensable condition of them both. These three (knowledge, conveying the message, and practice) cannot be separated from one another. Practicing with what one knows is an expression of respect for that knowledge. It is not only disrespectful but also blindness if a person knows Allah ﷻ but is not a proper servant to Him.

Islam is harmed more than what its adversaries can do when those who assume the duty of serving the faith cannot properly observe it at a personal level. This is what non-Muslims would say when they saw such Muslims who do not live by Islam, or those who are in the masjid physically as a formality but not really there in spirit.

People do not accept what they are called to, be it faith or anything else, when they are not put into practice by those who invite them, when they are not fully internalized and made a way of life. Historically, when Muslims had integrity of the heart and the mind, when our inside was in harmony with our outside, and when we internalized the message of the Qur'an, lived in compliance with Islam, and aspired to provide guidance for all humanity to righteousness and peace, people would acknowledge and embrace Islam even before we invited them.

Why should people join a community which is in discord, which barely knows its own religion, which leads a life indifferent to Allah ﷻ, and which is unaware of the content of its Holy Book? They look at the practice, mind, and heart of Muslims. What really makes a difference is when Muslims spend their nights in prayer, remembrance, and glorifications of Allah ﷻ, when they do not waste their time on useless things and spend every moment for the benefit of all. If Muslims could live their faith fully, people would run to embrace Islam. This is not the case, and so is the result. And non-Muslims have kept away from Muslims, at least for now.

Islam is a Divine system which integrates faith and practice. If belief constitutes one half of this system, the other half is putting it into practice. It is good to tell the stories of other people and what great believers they were—listeners might benefit from these stories and take lessons for their own lives. But telling these stories without practicing them in our own lives will not bring about the desired result. Islam is neither just to narrate the parables and stories of the saints nor just to listen to them. What befalls on us is to live the impeccable life described in them and to put it into action sincerely. Islam means both faith and practice. It is ineffective for those who do not accept it in this way to speak of Islamic service.

2.2. Awareness of the era

In our day and age, people's perspectives on life, things, and events have completely changed. Reason dominates as the main source of influence shaping these perspectives. Disbelief is speaking under the name of science and philosophy. In the face of this, believers must respond with the same, and this largely depends on knowing the culture of one's own era. Such knowledge, we may say, is the real knowledge. In fact, real knowledge is a distinctive characteristic of the believer.

A person who does not know his or her era is living in a dark tunnel. It is futile for such a person to try to tell other people something in the name of religion and faith. For the wheels of time and events will render them decrepit and ineffective tomorrow, if not today. For this reason, a Muslim should teach in accordance with the level of knowledge and culture of the day. I can certainly say that a spiritual guide and mentor who teaches others in this way can surpass even the saints and have a place right behind the Prophets in the Hereafter. This duty is so high, sacred, and honored. Reaching or acquiring this level is not easy, but it is as essential and necessary as it is difficult.

Teachers of faith who do not know their era are like those living under the ground, unaware of the world. Teachers or mentors of faith, however, have to be aware of the world as far as to outer space. While traveling intellectually in their head between the stars, they must observe Paradise with the eyes of their heart and spiritual faculties. Their mind and intellect must take them to the laboratory with Pasteur, into the depths of the existence with Einstein, and as they do so, they must always stand with their spirit behind the Messenger of Allah ﷺ to be infused and colored a few times a day with what he conveyed to us. To me, this is the true spiritual mentor or guide.

When we look at the Messenger of Allah ﷺ, we see that he engaged and dealt with his era in the proper way, so everything he conveyed to those around him was adopted and practiced wholeheartedly. In any case, no decree from Allah ﷻ is contrary to the events taking place in the universe—provided that one can comprehend the reason and meaning of existence and adjust and make their spiritual guidance according to it. The Companions, too, performed their call to faith with the lesson they received from the Messenger of Allah ﷺ, always taking into account the conditions of the day and the state of their interlocutors. Therefore, in a very short time, they had become powerful and wise enough to convince the multitudes to accept their message. All the great teachers and various saintly guides in the following centuries who were heirs to the Messenger of Allah ﷺ called people to faith in the same way. Imam Al-Ghazali, Imam Rabbani, and Mawlana Jalal ad-Din Rumi were some of those who successfully formulated their teaching in accordance with the mindset and culture of their era. This is why their influence continues even today. But unfortunately, when it was our turn, when the duty fell on us, we have turned our backs on knowledge like a prodigal heir and totally devastated the guidelines, customs, and heritage of being a true Muslim. We have thus become the victim of our own ignorance.

2.3. The relationship between the Qur'an and the heart

The spiritual mentor should tune his or her heart to the Qur'an. The Qur'an expresses this point as follows:

اِنَّ فِي ذٰلِكَ لَذِكْرٰى لِمَنْ كَانَ لَهُ قَلْبٌ اَوْ اَلْقَى السَّمْعَ وَهُوَ شَهِيدٌ

Surely in this is a reminder for whoever has a mindful heart and lends an attentive ear. (Qaf 50:37)

The Qur'an is a counsel, a reminder, a remembrance, and a warning. However, in order to be able to benefit from these aspects of the Qur'an, hearts must first be open to it. In order for the heart to be open, every person must set their eyes and ears on the Qur'an. This means turning entirely to the Qur'an; otherwise it is impossible to fully benefit from the Qur'an. Someone who cannot adjust their perspectives in this way cannot see the miracle that is the Qur'an. When they cannot see it, they deem no difference between the word of Allah ﷻ and the word of any human being. Someone whose level of thought has fallen so low cannot do anything in the name of Qur'an. The Qur'an says, "*This is the Book in which there is no doubt,*" and adds that it will bring "*containing guidance for those who are mindful of Allah*" (al-Baqarah 2:1-2):

ذٰلِكَ الْكِتَابُ لَا رَيْبَ فِيهِ هُدًى لِلْمُتَّقِينَ

The Qur'an is the Holy Scripture, the Word of Allah ﷻ. However, only those who are "*muttaqi,*" stated in the verse above, can benefit from the Qur'an to the desired extent. The word "*muttaqi*" is usually translated as the person who is mindful of Allah ﷻ, devout, pious, Allah-fearing, righteous, or conscious of Him. A *muttaqi* is also the one who knows the laws decreed in nature the best. An unserious person who would not be mindful of Allah, fearing and conscious of Him, can hardly benefit from the Qur'an, either. Their heart is no longer alert and alive: it is already dead, spiritually. The following verse sums up the attitudes of such people towards the Messenger of Allah ﷺ as follows:

يَنْظُرُونَ اِلَيْكَ نَظَرَ الْمَغْشِيِّ عَلَيْهِ مِنَ الْمَوْتِ فَاَوْلٰى لَهُمْ

... looking at you with a look of one swooning to death. That is, in fact, what is expected of them. (Muhammad 47:20)

How can someone who looks at the Prophet in this way understand anything from the Qur'an and its Messenger, the Prophet ﷺ? They can't. However, a person who tunes his heart in to the Qur'an hears and comprehends the events that continuously beat like the pulse of the universe in the beating of their own heart. How is this possible? Because he or she has established a necessary link, an accord, a unity, between the universe and oneself. People who cannot feel the pulse of events cannot do much in terms of spiritual guidance. In fact, this has much to do with trying to understand the Qur'an holistically.

It is an indispensable prerequisite for a spiritual mentor to apply the subjective and objective signs—namely the signs and events with respect to one's own self (the esoteric) and to the universe or general public (the exoteric)—to the verses of the Qur'an and then from them to make a composition, analysis, and synthesis. The guide becomes successful in his or her call to faith as much as they are successful at doing so. Otherwise, the rest is a waste of time for both themself and their interlocutors. Yes, spiritual mentors should be fully qualified with Islamic knowledge and attributes and must always behave with this moral distinctness, profundity, and excellence.

From such abilities to analyze the objective and subjective signs to other qualities, such as kindness, purity, decency, compassion, and self-discipline, all the attributes that make a believer a truly perfect believer, in the full sense of the word, should be the indispensable characteristics of a spiritual mentor. To put it another way, not every characteristic of a disbeliever is the attribute derived from unbelief, just as not every characteristic of the believer is an attribute of faith.[13] Perhaps the success of non-Muslims in various fields today lies in the fact that they are equipped with the attributes of believers. And naturally, the reason that believers sometimes suffer is because we have become tainted with the attributes of disbelief. However, each believer must attach the utmost importance to almost every quality of being a believer. Spiritual mentors or guides must exceed ordinary believers in representing these.

13 "While it is obligatory that all attributes of all Muslims are Muslim, in reality this may not always be so. Similarly, not all the attributes of all unbelievers have to be connected to unbelieving or arise from their unbelief. In the same way, all the attributes of all sinful transgressors may not be sinful, nor do they need always to arise from sinfulness. This means that an unbeliever's Muslim attribute prevails over a Muslim's irreligious attribute. Indirectly and due to the means, the unbeliever can prevail over the believer" (Nursi, *The Words*, p. 749–750. NJ: The Light, 2013).

The true believer is an embodiment of kindness, decency, and compassion. With these attributes, they consider the universe as a cradle of compassion and mercy, and a threshold of brotherhood and sisterhood. Their life should be in full self-control. Therefore, every moment of their life should be bright, luminous, and enlightened. They regard wasting time as the most terrible loss. They should not frequent places where people just idly waste time. The Messenger of Allah ﷺ never did so. Muslims should go to places of learning, worship, and educational institutions. The believer ought to be equipped with science, knowledge, and wisdom. They should be far from unmindful behavior and precarious and hazardous acts. They should carefully plan and program their personal and social affairs. They ought to perceive the relationship between cause and effect and cognitively grasp the essence of things. Individuals or nations are not superior on their own; they achieve progress when they adopt such attributes.

2.4. Legitimate means for legitimate ends

The spiritual mentor must be extremely careful and be sure that all the methods he or she uses are legitimate. A legitimate goal can only be achieved through legitimate means. Since what we aspire to must be a legitimate outcome, our means to acquire it must also be legitimate.

Our goal is the truth. We are averse to what is wrong and evil. We cannot use evil ways to which we are averse in order to achieve what we believe to be our rightful goal. If we do, then we are in denial of who we are and what we want to do. No lofty cause can be built on lies, and those that are built cannot live on for a long time. Allah ﷻ has always removed the blessings from the deeds of those who resort to that path. They may gather thousands of people in public squares and deliver fervent speeches to them, but they cannot have as much blessing as the spiritual mentor of a few devotees of Allah ﷻ gathered in a modest house and informing one another of the truth. While the former may count a thousand but is no worthier than one, the latter counts one but is likely to be as worth a thousand.

Hearts are in the hands of Allah. Making people accept what we say and are to say and helping them find the right path are entirely in the hands of Almighty Allah ﷻ. It can only be done by Allah ﷻ. Therefore, if our intention is to make people find the right path, we cannot use lies and exaggerated expressions; they will not contribute at all to achieving that goal. On the contrary, they would harm and hinder that goal.

We are obliged and responsible to perform our duty within the framework that Islam has drawn for us. We must never trespass into unlawful territory and use illegitimate means while serving Islam. Especially today, when lies and truths have become commodities sold in the same shop, we are obliged to speak truthfully, to act correctly, and to represent the truth honestly.

2.5. Compensation

The spiritual mentor should not ask for a return for the duty of "calling to good and preventing wrong." This return, be it a fee, wage, or any payment or reward, and be it material, immaterial, or spiritual, absolutely casts a shadow on one's sincerity and purity of intention. When a shadow falls, the sincerity and purity of intention are compromised, and the duty loses from its influence. Even spiritual pleasure and delight from mentorship should not be sought, let alone a material gain or remuneration. If a material benefit ever becomes a part of this service, the sincerity totally fades away, and the work done can no longer be called spiritual mentoring or guidance. The Holy Qur'an underscores this fact while quoting the universal statement made by all the Prophets as follows:

وَمَا اَسْـَٔلُكُمْ عَلَيْهِ مِنْ اَجْرٍ اِنْ اَجْرِيَ اِلَّا عَلٰى رَبِّ الْعَالَمِينَ

"I ask of you no wage for that (for conveying Allah's Message); my wage is due only from the Lord of the worlds." (ash-Shu'ara 26:109)

This verse is the clearest evidence for what we are talking about in this section. In fact, one feels in this statement an undertone of resentment which we may perhaps expound as follows:

I writhe in pain and suffering for you, for your sake. But you are calling me mad; you are insulting me and even pelting stones at me. You are trying to banish me from the people. I am going door to door trying to explain the truth and to convey His Message. You, however, are trying to close every door in my face. For all these pains you inflict on me and torments you make me suffer, despite all these trials and tribulations, I am not asking for any compensation, neither for this world nor for the hereafter. My reward will be given only by the One Who sent me with this duty.

These are almost the words, the experience, and the understanding of the duty of all the Prophets, from the Prophet Adam to Prophet Muhammad ﷺ, may Allah's ﷻ peace and blessings be upon them all.

When the disciples of the Prophet Isa (pbuh) came to Antioch,[14] the authorities of the land ordered that they immediately be arrested. A believer called Habib al-Najjar, who was respected and trusted by everybody in that region, heard about the incident, he came running and said the following to the authorities:

اِتَّبِعُوا مَنْ لَا يَسْـَٔلُكُمْ اَجْرًا وَهُمْ مُهْتَدُونَ

"Follow those who ask of you no wage (for their service), and are themselves rightly guided." (Ya-Sin 36:21)

As narrated in this verse, the Qur'an points out the two prerequisites that the spiritual guide must have. The first is that the spiritual guide themselves are to be rightly guided in what they are calling people to. The second is that they ask no compensation from anyone in return for the duty they perform.

If we expand on this, we can say that a Muslim who does not observe daily prayers cannot be a spiritual mentor. Because the words of a person who does not attentively, meticulously perform the daily prayers do not make and leave a lasting impact. Someone who lives on usury, bribery, or other unlawfully acquired earnings can never be a spiritual guide. How can those who live a wastefully luxurious worldly life be spiritual mentors when they are in need of such guidance for the sake of the Hereafter?

Those who do not determine their standard of living according to that of the majority of Muslims cannot be said to be following the path of the Prophet and his enlightened Companions. The behavior and utterance of such people is a lie, and no one can find the truth with a lie. It is absolutely impossible for those who have not found the truth themselves to make others find the truth.

Spiritual mentors are like a firm signpost that shows the truth. Anybody who sees the way they live can also immediately tell the em-

14 The Qur'an does not specify the city, but Antioch is commonly accepted to be the city mentioned in the verse. For more about the incident, see Abdurrazzak, Tafsiru's-San'ani 3/141; at-Tabari, Jamiu'l-bayan 22/159; Ibn Abi Hatim, at-Tafsir 10/3192.

bodiment of truth and righteousness in their faces. More precisely, those looking for a spiritual guide or mentor must see and find such embodiment before they follow a person.

Indeed, the Qur'an is a source of true faith and guidance for the followers who are *muttaqin*, conscious of Allah ﷻ (al-Baqarah 2:2). How can a person whose life does not fall within the framework determined by the Qur'an be able to benefit from this source of guidance? The true guidance is the Straight Path (*as-sirat al-mustaqim*) suggested by the Qur'an. A person who does not lead a righteous life cannot be said to have reached true guidance. Such a person's effort to guide others to the true faith is a complete self-contradiction. Therefore, the mentors and guides who are expected to be in the path of the Prophets should adhere to the Prophets while performing the duty of the Prophets. In particular, the following remarks by Bediüzzaman Said Nursi, a great mentor whose heart and mind were equally enlightened, should be heeded more than ever:

"*Misguided people accuse Muslim scholars of using knowledge to earn money and claim that they exploit religion and religious knowledge to make a living. We must refute such allegations through our deeds.*"[52]

Truly, we should refute critics by our truthful, righteous, exemplary deeds. The rest is empty talk and pointless.

There should always be a cadre of sincere volunteers on earth who will shoulder the service to Islam just for the love and sake of Allah ﷻ. These mentors exist for the happiness of humanity and should teach everybody how a real religious or spiritual mentor must behave by their exemplary action. This band of mentors must be so sincere and altruistic that the assets that will emerge when they die should only be sufficient for the shroud, and sometimes not even that much. Here are the believing hearts that adorn my dreams and here are the great patrons of the great service.

There have been many who talked empty rhetoric about practicing Islam in an ideal way. The way they behaved always disappointed people and belied their expectations. People can no longer bear and tolerate being further deceived. What they are looking for now is action not empty words. If the action confirms the words, then people embrace them and follow in their footsteps. Otherwise, they neither listen to nor respect those whose actions contradict their words.

To put it another way, people usually do not have a sense of belonging and trust with those who have a completely different lifestyle. On top of that, a believer's wisdom would not allow him or her to put faith in and develop a bond with those that appear to be contradictory. If you want to trust somebody, you first look at their lifestyle. If they live a modest life avoiding excesses and extremes, if what they say and do are not in contradiction, you will naturally believe in them. It is important to make sure whether a certain mentor checks the necessary credentials before one decides to follow in his or her footsteps. This is a fact proven by thousands of examples in history.

Looking for a guide or a spiritual mentor, one should consider not how eloquent a certain mentor speaks, but whether he or she lives a life like that of Prophet Muhammad ﷺ. Those who pay attention just to the outer form, and those who regard cunning words[15] as a big talent, will bring nothing but harm to the service of Islam. They are far from us in terms of spirit and so must we be from them.

Another point to consider is that a mentor can hardly teach anything to another person or people to whom he or she is indebted or who have done favors for him or her. It is for this very reason that the prominent teachers and guides of Islam, such as Abu Hanifa, Al-Layth ibn Sa'd, Sufyan al-Thawri, Fudayl ibn 'Iyad, Ibrahim ibn Adham, and many others, have been extraordinarily sensitive and scrupulous in this matter. It is again for this reason that their voices have survived centuries up until today and continue to influence people. The age of these incredible individuals was so prolific that so many of them were brought up in it to enlighten the world.

Once Sufyan al-Thawri was very sad. When he was asked why, he replied: "*I have been a teacher to so many people and I have taught them the sciences of the hadith, canonical jurisprudence, and commentary on the Qur'an. But I saw later that most of these people get a post as civil servants and join in the state bureaucracy. That makes me sad and worried. I am very afraid that on the Day of Judgment, I will be held to account for their mistakes and wrongful decisions.*"[53]

15 Translator's note: The author originally uses the word *"jarbaza,"* which means, "to show the lie as true by embellishing it, to rise to the top by deceiving with cunning words, to cover the truth with discursive acrobatics, and to cover up the truth with lies."

The letter Sufyan al-Thawri wrote to the Caliph Harun al-Rashid is well-known and shows exemplary behavior. When Harun al-Rashid became the caliph, he expected Sufyan, who was an old friend of his, to come to him to declare his allegiance. The Caliph had this right, one may assume, for the sake of such a sincere friendship. But Sufyan did not think like him at all. Harun could not wait any longer and sent a letter to Sufyan in which he wrote with a sense of resentment: "*Everybody came, pledged their allegiance, and went back with gifts. But my eyes have always searched for you.*"

Sufyan did not open the incoming letter himself. "*I cannot lay hands on a letter written by an oppressor,*" he said and made one of his students read it. Sufyan asked him to turn over the letter and write his answer on its back. His student hesitated, asking if that would be appropriate. Sufyan, the great man, replied to him: "*If this paper was a public property, we will send it back. If it was his own property, I have no money to spend for him ...*" He then dictated the following words: "*Harun, you became a caliph. You overspent the public money. You ask me to come in order to make me witness that. Remember, that one day you will appear before your Lord and be held accountable for all that you have done.*" A witness in the palace of Harun al-Rashid conveys to us the rest of the incident as follows:

Harun took the letter and read it. He sobbed. From that day on, he would ask his staff to read the letter for him at the end of each prayer, and he would say: "A friend like you should have been by my side during my rule, so that I would be saved from doing wrong ..."[54]

What was the source of Sufyan's courage to address the Caliph in this way? It was the fact that he did not surrender himself to transient worldly gains and that he had already overcome the temptations and vanities of worldly life. If he, too, had clung to the world like some of his contemporaries, he would not have been able to address the caliph in this way. Harun al-Rashid was a devout believer; he observed the daily prayers consistently, did voluntary fasting, and had gone on pilgrimage *(hajj* and *umrah)*. He was kind, compassionate and soft-hearted. However, in the face of some wrong spending, an old friend of his rebuked him.

Here, I would like to offer my advice to the generations from whom we expect the salvation of the humanity:

Hold your head high and preserve your self-esteem and dignity. Do not fall prey to certain centers of power. Even if you happen to accept certain jobs or duties for the nation or humanity, always be independent and act responsibly. Never be bound by limitations and conditions imposed by others, particularly in conveying the message and calling people to good. The principles laid down by Allah ﷻ are what really matters. Be a servant to Him alone! If you do so, your words will be effective and what you communicate to people will be accepted in the public opinion.

Allah Almighty ﷻ takes it on Himself to make sure your words do not fall on deaf ears, and He will reward you if you do not expect anything from others. Your recompense in this world is that your words are welcomed, and as for the Hereafter, you will be honored with Paradise and the Divine Beauty (*jamalullah*). If you do not act in this way, and if you demand something in return from the people, first of all your words will not have any influence, and then you will be deprived of the greatest blessings and favors of Allah ﷻ. Worldly posts and ranks are always temporary. They are not worth clinging to or being proud of. Any salary a person receives should not be soiled, tainted by morally dubious things or sources. I hope that one day the living standards change for the better and everyone will find a decent, legitimate way of earning a living.

Spiritual mentors should not be after any worldly status in return for this lofty service. For a more sincere fulfilment of this service, they should not even expect any *otherworldly* status, either. Mentoring several individuals is superior not only to any high official position but also to being, say, a saint. Teaching and guiding people to the right path is the essential duty of believers. No worldly or spiritual rank can surpass this.

In this respect, it would be foolish for the mentors to use their services as a means for worldly interests. Also, it would be unwise and unholy to use the good name or status attained by way of this mentorship for material benefits and worldly gains. It would be as foolish and stupid as to exchange priceless gold, diamonds, and gems for worthless shards of glass.

In a weak hadith, it is narrated that someone who acted this way during the time of the Prophet Musa (peace be upon him) was transfigured into a beast. Though this person used to speak of Prophet Musa and his greatness in every social gathering, Allah ﷻ transformed him into an abominable creature for he used all these for his own benefit. Allah ﷻ assured the Messenger of Islam ﷺ that his *ummah* will not experience such an end. He assured that literal metamorphosis, in terms of outward appearance, was abolished for his *ummah*. However, many people have suffered that end metaphorically, in terms of their moral character.

We pray to our Lord that He protects us and all spiritual mentors from being subjected to such a bad fate. Indeed, He is the All-Powerful One Who accepts and answers our prayers.

2.6. Knowing the person and empathy

a) Knowing the person

The spiritual mentor should be closely aware of what the person he or she is dealing with is thinking, understanding, and how he or she is responding to the things they are learning. The mentor should empathize, show consideration, bear with the person, and make allowances toward their mistakes.

A mentor should approach other believers with munificence while calling them to the good. As for misguided people, mentors may be able to have access to their hearts and minds if they approach them with foresight, prudence, sagacity, and tenacity, hoping that their message will be welcomed and embraced.

The mentor should know the situation of the mentee very well and strictly avoid behaviors and attitudes that are discouraging and may cause antipathy or dislike. First of all, the things presented by the mentor are all sacred notions. Mentors, whose duty is to make people love Allah ﷻ, His Messenger ﷺ, His Book and the Hereafter, should know what their duty is and adjust their behavior accordingly. Because any discomfort or inconvenience the mentee feels towards the mentor—Allah ﷻ forbid—may lead to a hatred of the things the mentor loves and is trying to convey. Being the cause of such hatred is the biggest loss, and if it stems from the mentor's personal state, he or she will bear the responsibility for it in the Hereafter.

The Messenger of Allah ﷺ conveyed the message so individuals wouldn't feel guilt. He did not confront disbelieving, erring, and sinning individuals as if they were already guilty. He would not address the disbeliever or the sinner directly and accusingly. Instead, he addressed his words to the whole community, to the public. Whenever he saw a mistake or defect concerning the details of a practice or teaching, he immediately would ascend the pulpit and speak to the whole audience. Now, let me illustrate this with a few examples:

A Companion of the Prophet was once saying his prayers too loudly and his hands were up in the sky but in an awkward way. This was against the manners of the prayer. However, instead of talking directly to him, the Messenger of Allah ﷺ addressed all those who were there:

"Don't trouble yourselves too much! You are not calling a deaf or an absent person, but you are calling One Who hears, sees, and is very near."[55]

Once, people complained to Allah's Messenger ﷺ about a certain imam whose prayers (*salah*) lasted so long that it became unbearable for them to pray behind him. The Messenger ﷺ grew displeased. Although he knew who the imam was, he did not warn him directly, instead he addressed the whole community in the masjid:

"O people! Why do you make people hate? Whoever among you leads the people in prayer, he should shorten it because among them are the old, the weak and the busy [who have urgent business to attend]."[56]

This was how the Messenger of Allah ﷺ dealt with people's mistakes. He wanted people to attain their salvation, and this is why he made it easy for them and offered his message in the most convenient way. He said, *"O People! Say, 'no Allah but Allah' and attain success."*[57] That "success" was why he was sent as a Messenger to humanity.

It is absolutely wrong to make people feel guilty for their past or present failures while trying to teach them something in terms of spiritual mentoring. Blaming them personally may undermine their dignity; this is why mentors should prefer to pronounce their warnings publicly to avoid finger-pointing. Just as everyone benefits from the rays of sun according to their own capacity and aptness, everyone can benefit from these enlightening words in proportion to their own aptitude, preparedness, and potentialities. Otherwise, it will be very difficult to repair the breaches and damages done in society.

b) Avoiding debates

If circumstances require the spiritual mentor to discuss an issue with the mentee, he or she should pay great care not to drag it into a debate. For it is generally the self or ego who speaks in a debate rather than the truth. When egos debate and attempt to defeat one another, it means that the occasion has been handed over to the devil in the name of truth. No matter how convincing and eloquent we may speak, it will not have the slightest effect and will not be well received. Debate is an inadequate forum for the truth. While we are preparing for the debate, we try to equip ourselves with ideas and arguments that would defeat "the opponent." Likewise, our mentee will be mostly in the same mood before and during the debate. He or she will definitely respond to what they will bring forth with his or her own counterevidence or counterarguments. So, the conversation will enter such a vicious circle that no conclusion will be reached even if the debate lasts for days.

It is true that our Prophet ﷺ was drawn to debate once or twice. It is also true that in those occasions, he tried to convince his interlocutor. However, the point to be considered here is that the demand for the debate came entirely from the other side.[58] In such a situation, of course, he did not have the option to not accept such invitations. If he were to remain silent against such challenges, the strength and morale of those who listened to Him could be shaken. Most of these people who came to the Prophet ﷺ to debate were again not persuaded but silenced by the evidence presented.[59] Being silenced does not mean they were guided to the truth.

Although our Prophet ﷺ came face to face with the learned men of the Bani Israil (the Children of Israel), no one among them embraced Islam after such debates. Yet, he was the Prophet for whom the universe was created and to whose heart all inspirations flowed like waterfalls. To put it another way, he was bestowed with countless blessings and miracles, or rather, he was always in contact with the Heavens or otherworldly wonders. However, those who were on the grounds of debate with him could not ever be drawn to the true faith; at most, they were just silenced with good arguments. Abdullah ibn Salaam was a prominent, respected scholar of the Jewish community of that era. But he came to the Messenger of Allah ﷺ not to debate but to verify what he knew as the truth.

"If this is the awaited person described in the Torah, I will believe him at once," he thought. No sooner had he seen our Prophet, Abdullah ibn Salaam realized that it was not the face of a liar and thus wholeheartedly embraced Islam.[60]

In the context of debate, Allah's ﷻ pleasure may slip from the mind and the heart. While debating, both the mentor and mentee would be under the pressure of their egos. And Allah ﷻ does not approve of a situation where the Divine approval is not taken into consideration, regardless of whatever is said there. A person's guidance to faith is completely in the hands of Allah ﷻ; it is certain that there will be no guidance at a time and place where His consent or approval is missing.

c) Freeing oneself from egotism and hubris

Egotism[16] and hubris are factors that hinder both guidance and its ensuing blessings. The mentor should get rid of this flaw and convey the message in a humble way. A mentor's humility helps save the mentee from prejudice and obstinacy. In fact, no one has the right and authority to be egotistical. That is, one should not overestimate one's own skills or characteristics, nor conceive that they are special or better. It is not rare that spiritual mentors fail in their teaching even though they use all their communication skills with eloquent and rhetorical words of wit and logic. It is not rare either that they might have a much greater influence when they are overwhelmed with humility under the heaviness of the duty and that they cannot utter even a few words properly. Allah ﷻ alone creates the light of faith in people's heart. It is Allah ﷻ alone Who guides people into faith. Allah ﷻ makes the mentor a means for people to attain faith.

d) Knowing the mindset of the mentee well

Spiritual mentors should fairly know about the mindset, worldview, or ideology of the mentee in advance. More particularly, there are many

16 Egotism and egoism are usually confused. Egotism refers to an overstated evaluation of one's skills, significance, and looks. It is about adoring oneself based on the misconception that one is special. Egoism, however, places self-interest at the center of one's moral compass.

groups who adopt different approaches at serving Islam. Acknowledging the existence of such approaches is totally different from approving or condoning them. Besides, not accepting the existence of something that already exists, or ignoring it, does not solve any problem. Therefore, spiritual mentors must always keep in mind that people listening to them may be affiliated with one of those groups or approaches. Being aware of this, mentors should not speak in a disparaging or condemning way about such communities; they should not backbite them. It is normal that every community considers its own way to be right and good, but they (communities) must also recognize others' right to exist and engage with them in good terms. Allah ﷻ does not approve of behaviors contrary to this, and He may cut His blessings of those who behave as such.

Spiritual mentors must respect all communities that serve the Qur'an sincerely and should also respect the wisdom of their interlocutors. The words they choose and say should be acceptable to everyone. For Allah ﷻ is not pleased with, or does not love, those who criticize and treat believers badly, who cut off relations with those who have established relations with Him ﷻ even if this connection is basic as belief in Him.

Getting in contact with almost everybody who has a relationship with Allah ﷻ shows the degree of a person's relationship with Allah ﷻ in a sense. Being aware of their relationship with Allah ﷻ might serve as a yardstick for us to adjust the level of our relationship with them. Based on this, mentors should invite people to faith itself, not to their own group or community. The most important factor that will unite different characters and members into a peaceful community—or into a coherent, united nation—must be the development of this consciousness.

Another way to understand the interlocutors is knowing their social status, cultural milieu, and educational level. This is crucial in terms of how the mentor can approach the mentee. Just as calling to good is a duty, so is knowing how to do it. For the sake of analogy, confronting a fully armed enemy is important, but it will surely end with your defeat if you confront them with a piece of stick. The situation is even worse if such a defeat will have devastating consequences for the whole Muslim world.

Knowing how to call people to good is one of the conditions, perhaps the most important one, of this duty. Just as we believe the necessity of this duty, so should we acknowledge that it also demands following a certain methodology. For instance, if the words we use in our teaching are far below or above the level of education of the interlocutor, this means we are not following a proper methodology and our teaching may not produce any positive result.

A proper methodology also demands a proper order of what we should be teaching. For instance, the virtues of the extra night prayers (*tahajjud*) are not the first thing to start teaching to a person who denies Allah ﷻ or is staggering with disbelief. That person needs to be informed of the principles of faith that have been fashioned in accordance with his or her mindset. Disbelief today originates from scientific perspectives, and so must teaching about faith be. Alas! So many mistakes and errors are being made towards the disbelieving because people dealing with them choose the wrong diagnosis and wrong methods of treatment for them.

Instead of dealing with and healing the heart of today's young generations, if the mentor deals with their outward appearance and look, with their clothing and hair styles, the mentor frightens them and pushes them away. Such mistakes in the technique of spiritual mentoring may result in the loss of people's eternal lives. Therefore, figuring out how and what you're going to prioritize in spiritual guidance is of the utmost importance.

When your mentees are interested in and always talking about positive sciences and engineering, you cannot approach them with a manual of religious worship and principles. This is not to undermine such manuals or books of catechism but to show how they're the wrong tools for this case. To give another example, if they do not believe in the Hereafter, it is pointless and a complete waste of time to tell them legendary stories of some saints. Even the most melodramatic of those stories would not have any influence, for people do not consist of emotions only; they also have a reason that needs to be convinced.

Sa'ad al-Din al-Taftazani[17] defines faith (*iman*) as a light Allah ﷻ sets in a person's heart. He adds giving convincing proofs as the duty of the mentor. It is such faith that will lead a person to commit righteous

17 One of the greatest Muslim scientists and Islamic scholars of the 14th century.

deeds and to live a whole faithful life. For those who leaped into faith with the impulse of their feelings in any given moment, it is very likely that they may leave it in another moment when they are overcome with another set of feelings that urge them in the opposite direction.

In hundreds of verses of the holy Qur'an, one may find references to many scientific and technological issues. Yet, the Qur'an is not a book of physics or chemistry or other physical sciences. With such references, the Qur'an encourages its followers to study these sciences which are needed for a comprehensive teaching of faith. It is difficult for a person who is not even a little familiar with the facts of astronomy and who has not read anything about biology to understand a great number of the verses of the Qur'an to the desired extent. Because there are such verses whose comprehensibility depends partially on the knowledge of these sciences. Here, I will not count all those sciences or scientific facts referenced in the Qur'anic verses but would like to emphasize that spiritual mentors today have to follow the science and technology of our century and at least have basic knowledge of as many of them as possible. Otherwise, their mentoring would be very limited and not comprehensive at all.

e) Knowing the culture of the age

Today, many people, be they young or old, are in a heartbreaking situation. This has partly stemmed from the miserable conditions of spiritual mentors who do not know the culture, worldview, and communication skills of the age they live in, and thus can hardly tell anything to their contemporaries. Nevertheless, assuming that we may cause more harm than good when we try to teach without proper understanding of our time, it is wrong to think that it is no longer our duty to call people to good and prevent wrong. This is not a duty to forgo; we would still be compelled to do it even if it would take travelling to the stars. We cannot sit still and do nothing when the minds of our young are confused with certain arguments of disbelief allegedly based on physics, chemistry, and astronomy.

It is incumbent on us to use the same contemporary methods and materials to take our generation's hand and lift them up, to heal their material and spiritual wounds. We have to raise them up so that they don't fall again, slip, and get trampled underfoot. Every event and every object in the universe are of a language telling us the truth; they are each a branch lowered down to save us. Those who believe in Allah ﷻ should know this language and hold on to these branches firmly. Otherwise, it will not be possible to understand Allah's ﷻ signs in the entire creation and the laws He established in nature. Individuals and nations that do not understand these signs and laws are bound to stay in deprivation. The Qur'an deals with and explains these signs in many of its verses. The person who turns a deaf ear to them, cannot be considered to have read the Qur'an in its true meaning even if they read it cover to cover every day. The Qur'an was sent for all its content to be pondered over in its entirety. Muslims who claim ownership of the Qur'an have to acknowledge what it is for in the first place.

No matter how blessed and sacred the truths we tell are, the effectiveness of spiritual mentoring is uncertain if it does not take into consideration the understanding, zeitgeist, and language of the time. Presenting religion and the Qur'an in an enigmatic way and covered in veils of mystery which cannot be reconciled with reason would only confuse the minds of young generations and push disbelievers further away. Unfortunately, we have seen, with a broken heart and weeping eyes, that teaching faith has been done this way for a very long time.

The Companions of the Messenger of Allah ﷺ were well above the cultural level of their time. They were able to explain the faith and how to practice it to their communities in the best possible way. After the Companions, many great individuals proved to be the leading figures in culture and learning. Everyone was impressed by the extraordinary intellectual capacity of Imam al-Ghazali, who was considered to be the renovator of his century. For centuries, al-Ghazali was admired even by Western scholars like H. A. R. Gibb and Ernest Renan, who praised his mastery of the culture of his time. Very much like him, Imam Rabbani, Mawlana Halid al-Baghdadi, and many others were early bloomers during their eras and brought light to their communities. Their teaching and guiding styles were also a reflection of their cultural level, and thus, what they taught resonated with the public conscience and was accepted.

f) Being accommodating

Spiritual mentors should be sensitive to the feelings and needs of others and try to be supportive, kind, and nurturing while helping them find the right path. Depending on the situation, the mentors may need to take a different approach to help others to get their spiritual needs met. They should be adaptable and accommodating because sometimes they may need to go down to the bottom of the cliffs, to take our generation's hand and lift them up, to heal their material and spiritual wounds, and to elevate them again. Sometimes they may need to go up to the heights to keep others in balance and harmony in their spiritual journey and to make them feel the sense of elation of progress and righteousness. It is quite normal for a spiritual mentor to have mentees at the either ends of the spectrum. This necessitates the mentor's cultural spectrum to be very wide and flexible. Otherwise, we cannot call them true mentors; they may block the path to real guidance and hinder progress. Such people had better step aside and open the way so that the real spiritual mentors come and give a helping hand to perplexed and troubled individuals.

About the troubled individuals who end up losing their faith, Bediüzzaman Said Nursi, one of the greatest mentors, who always felt the pain on their behalf, once said that if it was possible for a heart to physically explode out of sorrow, in the face of the unbelief of a young person, the heart of a believer must break into pieces.[61] Truly, this is the suffering heart. Without feeling a similar anguish in the face of a youth's unbelief, it is hard to qualify as an ideal spiritual mentor.

An ideal spiritual mentor is not only well-informed about their era, but they are also strong enough not to yield to worldly temptations. They are so altruistic that as they try to fulfill the duty of "calling to good and preventing wrong" not only worldly pleasures but even Paradise may temporarily slip from their minds. They have a pure heart with a selfless dedication to conveying the message. They try to do every duty that befalls them with such consciousness and sincerity. Then Allah ﷻ honors them with His support and success and enables them to convince the people around them.

Earlier, I pointed out the necessity of knowing the things the mentee needs. This is one of the duties of the mentor. Just as treating a disease without diagnosing it first is a big mistake, so is trying to provide spiritual healing without identifying the points of most suffering. It is necessary to note that every medicine would not cure every disease.

Nowadays some people are completely preoccupied with the economy, the importance of heavy industry, investments, or technology. They attribute the salvation of humanity to work only in this direction. I assure you, unless you deal with the generations to inform their minds and save their souls, unless you nurture them with morality and spirituality, and unless you let them flourish with the consciousness of the Hereafter, neither the factories you build nor your references to developed nations will be of any use for them to have a perfect character.

No promise of a luxurious life and fantastic thoughts can truly satisfy perplexed generations who have gone rebellious and rough—unless they are nourished spiritually. It is vain to think that the suffering of generations will be cured by economic solutions.

As Muslim communities lost the skill to speak in accordance with the requirements of the modern era, they have been brought down from the position of addressing and guiding others. Today they are in a state of just listening, without ever speaking. I wish they could have at least made a synthesis of what they are listening to. Have they been a fair listener? One seriously doubts that, too. However, we have in hand the Qur'an, the Miraculous Expression, which has the capacity and merit to challenge the entire universe and to appeal to all humanity. And again, we have in hand the immortal traditions (*sunnah*) of the Messenger of Allah ﷺ which interpret the Qur'an to us in the best possible way.

It is a pity that to this day we have not been able to benefit from them properly. We have not been able to attain the integrity of our hearts and minds and to immerse ourselves in the ocean of the Qur'an. Therefore, the Qur'an and the Sunnah are no longer telling us anything. As long as we do not change ourselves, their silence will continue, and today's Muslim will never be able to get out of the current chaos they are in.

The world is changing. Science and technology are developing at a dizzying pace. But what some of us are speaking today is not in conformity with the scales of developed nations. We are still stuck three centuries ago and cannot speak and appeal to today's generations. Of course, when this is the case, no one listens to or take heed of what we say.

g) Dealing with issues from contemporary perspectives

Today's spiritual guides and mentors should assess and explain the issues from the perspective of the era they are living in. They have to be not only familiar with the mindset and spiritual nature of the mentees but also aware of the problems gnawing away at their minds and souls. In such awareness and understanding, the mentors should convey what is needed so that their guidance is welcomed, accepted, and reciprocated both in the heart and the logic of their mentees. Mentorship done without such awareness would be like treating internal bleeding with a penicillin shot only.

The points raised so far are not mere abstract statements made by a person. They are conclusions derived from and confirmed by the Qur'an and Sunnah. Let me illustrate this with some examples.

اِقْرَأْ بِاسْمِ رَبِّكَ الَّذِي خَلَقَ

"Read in the name of your Lord Who created" (al-'Alaq 96:1) In this very first verse, the Qur'an draws attention to issues such as the creation of universe, laws in nature, the creation of man, and the origin of life and forms on earth. All philosophers, from Epicurus to Democritus, from Socrates to Plato, and to those who lived in the era of our Prophet, were all preoccupied with the subject of genesis and tried to study it. This means that throughout history, people had some knowledge of the first creation. They also knew that the human being originated from a drop of water or liquid, and that an embryo and fetus went through various stages in the mother's uterus. But the Qur'an treated the subject from a much broader perspective and said to human beings:

قُلْ سِيرُوا فِي الْأَرْضِ فَانْظُرُوا كَيْفَ بَدَأَ الْخَلْقَ

"Say: 'Travel through the earth and see how Allah originated creation'" (al-Ankabut 29:20). It said so because no one so far had been able to explain with human knowledge and ideas how the creation had originally started, how Allah ﷻ brings life into a being, and then how Allah ﷻ will bring forth the other (second) creation (in the form of the Hereafter). It is not possible to explain the creation without attributing it to Allah ﷻ.

The Qur'an sets out by explaining this difficult and astounding matter which everyone is incapable of explaining by themselves. Thus, the Qur'an draws our attention to the signs and proofs of creation. Those signs are like an ornamented necklace put on the neck of the universe by Allah's ﷻ omnipotence and will. They are at the same time an exhibition for us to see and observe, and a book for us to read and recite. Indeed, we are created in a position to see, analyze, and evaluate this book, this exhibition, this necklace through the given signs. It is unlikely for us to perceive the things and events within the universe otherwise.

It is against common sense if spiritual mentors try to maintain their bond with mentees by way of emotional ties only; that would contradict the natural law decreed in the world, nor would it have any lasting results. Having good opinion of each other and being hopeful are fine, but they are not enough all by themselves to allow us to walk straight. Emotions and good will may not last forever and could break down at any instant. However, if the mentors can foster both the mind and heart of their mentees and facilitate their preparedness for the requirements of the time, nurture them to adapt themselves to changing circumstances of the day, the bond or attachment between them will never get loose, time will not erode it, and trials and tribulations will only serve to strengthen ties and to reinforce their will and commitment to call people to good and prevent evil.

One topic I would like to address at this point may sound only slightly relevant, but it is as serious as the general theme of our book at hand: there are many religiously observant families whose children are not practicing Muslims at all, if not entirely disbelieving. On the other hand, there are many irreligious and unbelievers whose children are devout Muslims. Some of them even have to endure the oppression of their family members and are in search of options for more favorable grounds and conditions to be able to practice freely. Such incidents are real and will also happen in the future. One might speculate that such pious families are not able to explain Islam to their children in a way that fits their spiritual and mental nature. Growing up in a pious family, the child does not have many outside options for the issues he needs and expects to be clarified. The religious culture they receive from their family could only bring them to a certain point. A hesitation or a doubt in the head of this child or this young person, who already has gaps in their soul and mind, causes him to slip away and leave the religion.

I once visited such a family. The father was so devout, so pure in heart that I nearly felt ashamed of myself. But a little later, his son, a university student, entered the room. When he spoke, I immediately understood that he was a disbeliever. How I would wish, my inner voice said, that the father was able to raise his son as a believer instead of himself being this pure and devout.

Contrary to the above example, a child raised in an irreligious family may feel the need to ask others about the problems they cannot escape and solve by themselves. If they can find somebody who can provide convincing answers to their questions according to the circumstances of the day, the child may love and adopt faith. However, the religiosity of the previous child who grew up in a religious family did not go beyond imitation. And after some time, his imitative faith is not helpful in the face of outer challenges.

Now I would like to turn back to the main subject.

h) What to teach and how to teach it

Sometimes the level of knowledge and understanding of the mentees requires us to adjust our message and style accordingly. As a matter of fact, addressing human beings by "descending" to their mental and comprehension level is, as it were, one aspect of the ethics of Allah ﷻ. The Messenger of Allah ﷺ calls us to assume the ethics of Allah ﷻ.[62] The Qur'an is the Divine Word, which attunes and descends to the mind of the human being from its opening chapter to the end. If the Qur'an had not been attuned and adapted to the limited mind, intellect, and capacity of the human being, we may, perhaps, not have comprehended any of it.

If Allah ﷻ had spoken in the Qur'an with the speech He ﷻ spoke to Prophet Musa on Mount Sinai, we would not be able to carry that weight. And again, if the Qur'an had been revealed in a style that only the great geniuses and masterminds would have understood, ninety-nine percent of people would not be able to benefit from it. The Qur'an is far from being an incomprehensible book—in His address to people in the Qur'an, Allah ﷻ speaks not only in the language of His Majesty and Lordship, but also, in accordance with His Divine Will, He takes into consideration the capacity of His interlocutors. Besides, His Divine Speech is not limited to the Qur'an; who knows what other kinds of words and manner of speech becoming to His Majesty there are, but we do not know them.

What we do know is that in line with His Divine Oneness He has always addressed human beings according to their level of comprehension and understanding.

We find in the Qur'an a reflection of our own comprehension. The Qur'an speaks to everyone according to their own level. No matter what their comprehension level is, every person feels that their own spiritual state is being depicted and addressed in the Qur'an—as if someone very close and familiar to them speaks about all their personal secrets.

It is quite normal for this to be the case. For the Qur'an is the Word of the All-Mighty, who created human beings. It is the Word of the Omniscient Creator, who knows and watches the human heart at every moment.[18] Allah ﷻ created the human being, brought them into the corporeal world, and gave them their spirit from the Realm of Divine Command. Yet, neither can the spirit fully comprehend the body it is placed in, nor can the body fully comprehend the spirit it lives by. The One who created and united both of these into a whole human being is the One who knows them best. And the Qur'an is the speech of the One who is All-Knowing ﷻ.

With its content, this Divine Word is a source of true faith and guidance; with its attribute of speech, it is a fountain of learning for all spiritual guides. We will always refer to it to learn how to address our interlocutors.

It is a fact that the Qur'an addresses different levels of human understanding since it is the Word of Allah ﷻ Who created the human being in the best mold of the manifestation of His Names and Attributes. Thousands of scholars have manifested their own levels and differences of understanding in their reflections and considerations on the Qur'an. This was also the case in the era of the Messenger of Allah ﷺ —in other words, the Companions' level of understanding and perception of the Qur'an was not the same. Not all of the Companions understood the

18 Allah calls Himself *"Al-Muhaymin"* in the Qur'an (al-Hashr 59:23), which is mostly rendered in English as He is the Guardian, the Witness, the Overseer, the One Who ensures the wellbeing of creation, Who knows all secrets and what is even more secret than secrets, Who sees all things, both hidden and seen and what lies behind them.

Qur'an at the same level. And that difference of levels was not an obstacle preventing them from benefitting from the Qur'an.

A Bedouin living in the era of the Messenger of Allah ﷺ could come and listen to the Qur'an and benefit from it with both his heart and mind. The great poets who lived in the same period and whose poems were hung in the Ka'ba were also able to benefit from the Qur'an in the same way. Labid was just one of them, and he had given up writing poems after having listened to the Qur'an.[63] Hansa was one of the best and most powerful poets of the time. She had fallen in love with the Qur'an. They were the top masters of the Arabic language and literature in terms of form, style, content, and artistry.[64] They were the interlocutors of the Qur'an in this aspect, and the Qur'an satisfied them more than enough with both their minds and hearts. Many great minds such as Ibn Sina, Ibn Rushd, Al-Farabi, Imam al-Ghazali, Fakhr al-din ar-Razi along with Abu Hanifa, Imam al-Shafi'i, Imam Ahmad ibn Hanbal, Imam Malik, and many other magnificent minds whose names we cannot cite here, were all interlocutors of the Qur'an, raised and instructed by it. This means that the Qur'an addressed them in the same way, too.

The Qur'an indeed takes into consideration the level of intellect of human beings in every field and addresses them according to their understanding. This aspect of the Qur'an is so brilliant, so colorful that everyone listening to it intently thinks that he or she is the only person it addresses. This includes scientists, too. Every day, we are learning about new, mind-blowing developments in science and technology. New scientists are emerging almost in every field with much broader knowledge than before. In order to develop the latent abilities that the Creator has placed in their nature, while gaining skills through working on the natural laws that the Creator has established in the universe, scientists always find the Qur'an, the eternal word of the same Creator, as their biggest helper.

Under the enlightening dome of the Qur'an, thousands of people of science benefit from it at different levels. Chemists, physicists, astronomers, biologists, and even mathematicians can all listen to the Qur'an as if it is speaking in the language of their own field. According to an agriculturist, the Qur'an speaks of agriculture almost from beginning to end. According to a physician, the Qur'an is like an undisguised, speaking, illuminating, and guiding center of knowledge—much better than state-of-the-art research centers. The same is true for other scientists and branches of science, too. That is to say, the peasant who manually plows a field and the scientist who engages in deep-space exploration by pressing a button can also be the interlocutors, addressees of the Qur'an.

With such a profound capacity, the Qur'an educates us regarding the human condition. The Qur'an mentions every science in a concise way as in an encyclopedic entry. But it is not an encyclopedia. It is rather a guide that is meant to elevate the human being from the earth to the heavens and from there to eternity. While doing all this, it also teaches a methodology. A spiritual mentor who is familiar with this Qur'anic methodology should always take into consideration the state and level of the interlocutor and speak accordingly. Although this seems to be a difficult task, it is extremely useful and necessary.

Some try to speak ambiguously or too philosophically so that they appear educated; this is a grave error. What really matters in spiritual mentorship is to deliver the message as comprehensibly as possible. Therefore, the message needs to be crystal clear and smooth. Conversations should be accessible to all.

Today's young are strangers to religious terms and phrases. It is necessary to speak to them in a language that they can understand. We can exemplify this by how we communicate with children. We conform to a three-year old's way of walking, we speak the way he or she speaks, we laugh the way he or she laughs, and we behave the way he or she behaves. Therefore, it is imperative that the understanding of the interlocutors is taken into consideration in spiritual mentoring. Otherwise, the grandiose or pompous words we use while speaking to children will only make them laugh and will not increase their knowledge.

While we are telling our young generations about Islam, we do not have to use the heavily philosophical language of Bergson, Pascal, Plato, and Descartes. We need Prophet Muhammad's ﷺ method of guidance. The Messenger of Allah ﷺ always attuned with, conformed to, and cared about the comprehension level of his audience—an audience that included everyone. If need be, he was being a child for children, a young person for the young, and an elderly person for the elderly. This was nothing but the Divine ethics, which the Prophets adopted and implemented in their teaching.

In a quote attributed to the Messenger of Allah ﷺ, he says, *"We, the assembly of Prophets have been commanded to speak to the people according to their level of intelligence."*[65] In another statement, he said, "Speak to the people only according to their level of knowledge—understanding."[19] By commanding us to do this, he informs and reminds us of an indispensable precept in conveying the message and spiritual guidance.

Whenever the Prophets spoke to people, they spoke according to their individual level of intelligence. They took into account the level of their aptitude and spoke to them in the way that best suited the people's intelligence.

2.7. The inter-play of faith, spiritual mentoring, and action

a) Spiritual mentoring and life

The principle of "talk the talk and walk the walk"—in other words, "teach what you practice, and practice what you teach"—should be one of the most important principles of a spiritual mentor. For, first and foremost, the mentor himself or herself is on the path of becoming a true believer. A true believer means the person who has attained their inner and outer integrity. There should not be any internal and external contradiction or conflict in the life of such a person. Dual living is an outright attribute of hypocrisy. This blameworthy attribute can never be found in a true spiritual mentor, nor should it be. Being a believer means a mentor occupies the supreme moral horizon of telling, every time and everywhere, only the things he or she does and lives.

If the mentor "talks the talk but does not walk the walk," that is, if they do not live in a way that agrees with the things they say, if they themselves do not put their own words into practice first, and if they do not lead by example, they will have no positive influence or effect on the people. Allah ﷻ does not bestow favor, blessings, and influence on non-sincere words and behaviors. Although sometimes there is some influence and success in the services of people who are partially sincere or

19 Abu Dawud, adab 20; Ibn Asakir, Tarihu Dimashk 42/523. Some other reports attribute this statement to Ali (r.a.).

not sincere at all, this success arises entirely from the lack of alternatives and is temporary. Sometimes such a situation takes place either because there are no more sincere people at that moment, or because the sincere ones have not yet been able to become a center of attraction.

In this respect, the fate of the insincere is to fade away or vanish when the day comes. This is how the Divine law has always been. The temporary success of these half-sincere or insincere people should not mislead the people of faith and wisdom.

A number of temporary successes for both the capitalist and communist worldviews in the last two centuries can serve as a good example of this. Both systems emerged as alternatives to each other. These systems have brought about exploitative and deceptive orders since there was no better and sincere alternative when they appeared. Today, however, we can argue that there are sincere, vigilant, and well-qualified alternatives emerging. They are expected to prove better alternatives to these exploitative, unfair, and abusive systems which are doomed to be replaced by truth, sincerity, trust, justice, ethics, and respect. Let's prove with our practice, action, good example, and sincerity that the teachings and guidance of true believers of Islam can become an acceptable, constructive, and successful alternative.

***

"Teaching what one practices, and practicing what one teaches" is possible when one can hold oneself to account and reach self-awareness. People who are stuck with their corporeal nature and who have not attained a certain maturity and consistency in their lives are not free from living in dualism. They can neither behave as they are, nor can they ever be as they behave. The qualities they exhibit among people—such as respectability, maturity, and stability—consist mostly of pretexts and artificial behaviors and have been found to be unwelcome. When they are by themselves, they are quite light-minded, offhand, and frivolous. These imply immaturity, inadequacy, and inconsistency on their part. The elimination of such negative attributes undoubtedly depends on a sound belief in, strong trust in, and a serious obedience to, the Almighty Creator.

In the life of a spiritual mentor there should be no difference between their behavior in public and in private. When they are alone, they must continue to behave the same way they behave when they are among others and strive to be sincere in all their actions. There should be no contradiction in their individual and social behaviors. Their nights must be as illumined as their day, and their days must be so bright as to give luster to the sun. They should not take for granted even a small mistake they committed as a result of carelessness; they should be seriously upset about it. They should feel ashamed and therefore refrain from talking about prayer in general on the morning of the night which they did not illuminate with vigils and prayers. They should weep and wash away with tears the dirt of an unlawful thing caught in their eye. Something unlawful or doubtful they eat should hurt their stomach for days. They regret any deviation from the right path so much so that they feel the flames of Hell in their soul.

No matter how attractive and how seemingly necessary a person's thoughts and ideas are, if they are not put into practice by the person themselves first, they can hardly receive the desired level of public acceptance. For the words spoken are not acknowledged in the conscience of the speaker. It is desiring the impossible to expect public acceptance for an idea which is not first acknowledged in the speaker's conscience.

b) Criteria

One dimension of the duty of spiritual mentoring and guidance in a Muslim society is that it actually sets a standard and criterion for sincere faith. Taking that as a measure, Muslims should organize their days accordingly and spend their nights reflecting on how to fulfill this responsibility. Going to the mosque once in a while, having fulfilled the Pilgrimage, or participating in religious events are not insignificant, but the real measure is how much one is dedicated to communicating the message. The true mentors should be very wary of any behavior that destroys the consciousness of conveying the message and mentoring spiritually. They should also avoid all behaviors that turn mentoring, guidance, and rituals into mere formalism and ceremonialism. Some religious activities, festivities, or formalist behaviors may be a source of consolation for some people, but they are far from being a standard or a measure for the entire society. In fact, one of the main reasons that societies are corrupted and weakened is the lack of performing the duty of "calling to good and preventing wrong" in a conscious and systematized way.

Today, this sacred duty must be accepted as an inherent debt and liability on each and every individual. When it is not assumed as such, many people's weaknesses will expose them to vortexes of mischief which will first destroy individuals and then collapse a whole society.

Let me emphasize once more that this duty is, first and foremost, a matter of faith, and those who have supported it up to now have always been people with strong faith. This will be so tomorrow, too.

If a few people in a large community takes a small step of "calling to good," and it eventually turns into a major movement embraced by hundreds of thousands of people, this cannot be explained by anything but their sincerity and strong faith. Without a doubt, the most remarkable characteristic of this movement would be that it is far from formalism and ceremonialism. Any movement that has come to being without toil and suffering cannot avoid being formalist and ceremonialist. Likewise, no movement that is identified with ceremonialism has tears, intellectual effort, trials, and tribulations at its beginning. Such movements do not last, nor do they have sincerity, love, and inclusiveness.

To sum it up, spiritual guides must fine-tune their every action and behavior according to their mentoring life. If he or she visits somewhere, they must go there with the intention of calling people to good. Their daily deeds and engagements should not be solely for personal pleasure or amusement. They even organize meeting their natural needs in a way that they become a means to fulfill this duty. They live with the consciousness that one day will come, and they will account for every breath they take. This is the way of the Prophets, the righteous ones, saints, and martyrs. They always taught what they practiced, and they always practiced what they taught. As to the hypocrites, they did not practice anything, but they still taught it, and they ignored what they taught. Every passing day they further deviated from the path of virtue—and also dragged those who followed them to the devastation.

Allah ﷻ addressed Isa, whom He sent as a teacher to human beings, in the following way: "*O Isa, son of Maryam! Advise yourself before you advise others; otherwise, be ashamed before Me.*"[66] In fact, this address is not to Isa as a Prophet alone, peace be upon him. Here, Isa was spoken to in relation to his mission of guiding humanity to truth. Whoever is in a position to teach others and guide people to truth, be it a Prophet or someone else, must practice what they teach so their teaching can have an effect on others. The Qur'an states this very clearly, "*Do you enjoin upon people godliness and virtue but forget your own selves, (even) while you recite the Book? Will you not understand and come to your senses?*" (al-Baqarah 2:44). The Divine Revelation advises us to start giving advice to one's self. How can we tell people to do what is right and forget to do it ourselves, even though we recite the Scripture? Have we no sense?

This verse was then a direct warning against the Children of Israel, and it is now an indirect warning to Muslims. As mentioned before, not doing what one says is a sign of hypocrisy and deception. Especially in times of decline, we witnessed the ineffectiveness of the people who behaved like so, and the general public rightly didn't trust them.

There have been many individuals who engaged with Islam intellectually and even represented Islam, who spoke about Islam and put forward new ideas at an academic level. So many of them have vanished without leaving a trace because they did not live by what they said, nor were their words rooted in faith. These people used to talk about "the Straight Path," and they claimed to be guiding people to the truth. Yet, a mild wind and tremor were enough to cause them to topple down. They even denied all they had said before and became ardent defenders of the opposing ideas. Consequently, they perished into the blue. But it is a pity that they ruined a civilization along with themselves, too.

c) Hardships

The duty of conveying the message and spiritual guidance is interwoven with trial and tribulations, and this is a work of Divine providence. We show much more care and protection for things we have obtained through hardship. Something that is achieved easily is also lost easily, just as the riches that are not based on difficulty, hard work, and fatigue may be consumed any moment. If fulfilling the duty of spiritual guidance were easy, so would be the risk of losing it, which would mean losing humanity's most fundamental purpose and assurance of existence. Such a loss renders human existence on earth meaningless. People must comprehend the essentiality of this sacred duty which brings meaning to their existence on earth.

It is not rare that many spiritual guides have been persecuted throughout history and in our day. Some of them had to suffer this under brutal regimes for so long that prisons became like a home for them. They suffered all kinds of pain and insults. Many among them could never return home after they were taken away, unjustly arrested. Others bid farewell to their families as they left home every morning, knowing that could be the last time they saw one another. Yet, they still endeavored to do their best under such circumstances. And soon their honest and sincere efforts began to bear good fruit. Their achievement is surely credited to the Infinite Mercy of Allah ﷻ that has come to rescue them and us in response to their suffering. What they have accomplished is so precious that no one has the right to squander this blessed heritage. Today, believing men and women are obliged to embrace and support this duty of spiritual guidance with the same level of dedication.

I had previously noted that fulfilling this duty is a matter of faith. Every individual who intends to preserve the faith must also be determined to keep it alive. They must embrace, support, and protect this way of serving Allah ﷻ at least as much as they care and protect their home, family, and business. Otherwise, it is not possible to be safe from the fate some ancient civilizations suffered.

The spiritual mentors must often remind themselves that they are likely to encounter all kinds of hardships and therefore be ready to endure them. They must be of firm conviction that success in spiritual guidance is more likely to come after going through many hardships and trials similar to what former teachers and guides of the past went through. This duty is not easy, and they must be willing, ready, and committed to overcome the difficulties in advance. If they experience ease and comfort, they must be thankful to Allah ﷻ for it and move forward faster.

The true believer is a sincere person. Practicing in one own's life what one teaches, or teaching what one practices in his or her own life, is a sign of sincerity. The opposite state is considered a characteristic of a liar and hypocrite. If a person talks about religion, faith, and the Qur'an and explains Islam to others at every opportunity, then his or her life must be aligned with the measures and principles of the words coming out of his or her mouth. There should be no room for sin in their lives; or at least they should regard sin as a potential cause for eternal suffering in their soul. In other words, if they happen to commit a sin, they must keep in mind that it will remain somewhere in the deepest corner of their conscience and will hurt them as a scorching torment. And in fact, no sin should remain in their soul for long.

The spiritual mentor does not look at the unlawful, does not touch the unlawful, and does not walk on an unlawful territory. Their night is as bright as their day, and their prayer rug should be in love with their prostrations at nights. You would never hear them say, "I missed my morning prayer today," for they would not. If they miss the morning prayer unintentionally, the rest of the day passes with a heavy resentment. They are so overwhelmed by this that you would notice their ensuing lack of enthusiasm on that day.

d) Hypocrisy

Self-supervision and self-accounting are two of the major principles that keep a spiritual mentor in action. Mentors must always control their inner self, keep their feelings and imaginations checked, and try hard to first have their teachings firmly settled in their own soul. If they have not internally attested to the truth of what they will be teaching, they should avoid teaching it to others. This avoidance does not hinder conveying the message; on the contrary, it encourages and enhances one's consciousness to convey the message and mentor people. The fear of falling into hypocrisy and resembling a hypocrite brings them constantly to earnestness and sincerity.

The Messenger of Allah ﷺ made the following statement about those who regard conveying the message and spiritual guidance only as verbal or dialectical: "*What I fear most about my ummah is the hypocrites who speak elegant words.*"[67] This is a chilling statement that causes one to tremble. For, everyone can be in a position to speak with others about Allah ﷻ and faith; thus, this statement is a reference point for all to scale up and prevent compromising their spiritual mentoring.

There are many warnings similar to the hadith above. Yet, we often encounter many who wander in the valleys of hypocrisy. We see such people often writing in columns and speaking on TV channels. But they live a life far from what they speak; their actions and behavior are far from what religion teaches. They talk about the faith and the Qur'an, but prayer is nowhere to be seen in their lives, and their hearts are insincere and dubious. Poor souls! They do not know that ninety percent of religion is related to the individual himself. Unless they observe that ninety percent, such individuals are considered to be a mere windbag or a fervent dialectician.

While listing the basic qualities of a spiritual mentor, the Qur'an also points to the characteristics of the hypocrite. Because what a good mentor should not do and stay away from is as equally important as what they should be doing. The Qur'anic account of hypocrites describes their qualities in such a style that believers are discouraged from them. It exposes them down to their inner considerations, feelings, and intentions. Sometimes it describes even their physical qualities, like their height, posture, as well as temperament and grumpy nature. For example, look at the style in this verse:

وَإِذَا رَأَيْتَهُمْ تُعْجِبُكَ أَجْسَامُهُمْ وَإِنْ يَقُولُوا تَسْمَعْ لِقَوْلِهِمْ كَأَنَّهُمْ خُشُبٌ مُسَنَّدَةٌ يَحْسَبُونَ كُلَّ صَيْحَةٍ عَ
لَيْهِمْ هُمُ الْعَدُوُّ فَاحْذَرْهُمْ قَاتَلَهُمُ اللّٰهُ أَنَّى يُؤْفَكُونَ

When you see them, their outward form pleases you, and you give ear to their words when they speak. (In reality) they are like blocks of wood propped up and (draped over) in striped cloaks. They think (being themselves treacherous) every shout (they hear) to be against them. They are the enemies themselves, so beware of them. May Allah destroy them (they are liable to destruction by Allah)! How they are turned away from the truth! (al-Munafiqun 63:4)

As is seen in the verse above, they are described and presented to us in general terms in such a way as to reveal their characteristics and nature. In other words, the Qur'an captures them in such an all-in-one picture with their manners, posture, behaviors, way of speaking, and coquettish behavior that you do not need further description. They know how to gather people around them with their gestures, eloquence, and rhetoric and drag masses behind them like flocks. However, they are as worthless as hollow pieces of timber propped up, unable to stand on their own, serving no useful purpose at all. They are like the wood draped over and thus concealed by a striped fabric, concealing their true nature. They are your enemies, so beware of them! The Qur'an uses these words for every one—old and new—who speaks a lot in the name of religion and nation but in truth does not do anything. The Qur'an seriously warns of the threat of such hypocritical people so that they do not compromise the truth and clear the path for falsehood. Do not cause mischief!

These manners and behaviors are described as signs of hypocrisy. Every spiritual mentor serving the truth should be afraid of these weaknesses and shun them. Anyone may fall into such setbacks at any moment without being aware of it. Therefore, those who are performing the duty of conveying the message and spiritual guidance need to be very careful and meticulous.

e) Adherence to Allah ﷻ

The more sincere the mentor is, the more effective their words and actions become. If there is no sincerity, the beauty and magnificence of speech, words, and expressions alone do not produce the desired result. Being guided into the true faith does not have much to do with our words and expressions alone. For one thing, guidance is first and foremost in the hands of Allah ﷻ. It is Him Who can guide one into the true faith. Guiding another person or people into the faith does not rest with us. All that we have to do is "convey the Message," and Allah ﷻ will guide whom He wills, and He has the ultimate wisdom—He knows best those who are the guided and who deserves to be guided. If He does not will and decree it, it is not possible for anyone to be instrumental in guiding people to the faith:

اِنَّكَ لَا تَهْدِي مَنْ اَحْبَبْتَ وَلٰكِنَّ اللّٰهَ يَهْدِي مَنْ يَشَاءُۚ وَهُوَ اَعْلَمُ بِالْمُهْتَدِينَ

You cannot guide to truth whomever you like, but Allah guides whomever He wills. He knows best who are guided (and amenable to guidance). (al-Qasas 28:56)

The main issue for believers, then, is to adhere to the Almighty Creator, to be in connection with the Sovereign, the Sultan of sultans. The key to all the treasures, hidden or open, is in His hands. Guidance to the true faith is the biggest treasure. Of course, the key to this treasure is in His hands, too. Therefore, while the mentor is telling people something with all his or her sincerity, it is essential that they rely on Allah's ﷻ Omnipotence. By not following this path, so many wonderful minds, who were highly talented speakers, have lived and passed in our communities, but they have not been able to tell anything serious even to a few people. The reason for this failure was that they were not sincere in what they were doing. They placed their self at the center of everything and attributed every outcome to themselves. Some among them were genius at delivering a speech. They had the potential to drag thousands of people behind them. However, they were stricken by hypocrisy; thus, they could hardly obtain any result. Their actions spoke contrary to their professed attitude. Some of them used to speak of daily prayers even though they did not offer a prayer. Some of them used to mention the virtues of Islam though they did not live by it. Their tongue was like that of the nightingale, singing beautifully, but their heart was beating with hatred and malice. Probably because of this, in the Qur'an, hypocrisy is treated as the most horrible and disgusting of all degrees of corruption.

Every sincere spiritual mentor should always take refuge in Allah so as not to fall into the pit of hypocrisy and beg for sincerity. Guidance is in the hands of Allah. Just as He is the One Who gives humans the strength of our physical body, He is also the One Who bestows sincerity in our hearts. So the mentor should not credit himself or herself and claim ownership of any of their good works; they should never say, "I did it..., I made it..."

The integrity of faith through words and actions is the most ideal form for a believer within the measures set by the Qur'an. Maintaining this balance is an important factor in a mentor's effectiveness. It is wrong to believe that you do not have to practice what you preach or that you do not have to avoid sins as long as you are striving in the path of Allah. Such thoughts are the whisperings of the devil and have nothing to do with Prophet Muhammad's way and spirit, peace be upon him.

Many modernist minds emerged in our time with many fanciful ideas. These minds have the brilliance of speech to convince others that white is black. They are always talking about Islam everywhere, but we see that there are not even a handful of sincere believers behind them. Because they are not truehearted and sincere. They speak a lot, they tell a lot, and they even engage in some struggles. But they have not been able to internalize the Islamic faith and practice as much as they claim to. Their lifestyles reflect not the truthful aspects of the West, but its wrongful aspects. Thus, they alienate the masses while allegedly informing and guiding them. At the same time, they are turning themselves into strangers within their own communities.

The main reason for all these contradictions is their failing to understand and honestly practice Islam although they read and philosophize on it. In other words, it is a kind of overt opposition or betrayal of the cause they are striving for through their inconsistent behaviors and actions. In response to such a mentality and attitude, the Qur'an had the Prophet Shu'aib speak in the following way:

وَمَا اُرِيدُ اَنْ اُخَالِفَكُمْ اِلٰى مَا اَنْهٰيكُمْ عَنْهُ

I do not want to do what I am forbidding you from. (Hud 11:88)

He means: "I am not thinking of any worldly gain, unlawful provisions, or profiting from what I forbade you. I do not forbid you from something and at the same time I contradict my prohibitions in secret behind your backs, doing what I have forbidden. I am not thinking of taking interest or bribes while I am saying these are unlawful." While depicting the society he lived in, Prophet Shu'aib told this to give assurances of his own veracity, righteousness, truthfulness, and legitimacy. These are assurances for every Prophet, too. It is not possible for a Prophet to do the opposite of what he tells his community to do. In other words, those acting in contradiction to their message cannot ever be a Prophet.

Of course, these are also essential, indispensable points for all those who perform the duty of spiritual mentoring and guidance. While the Prophet Shu'aib struggled against the mentality of his society, he endowed us with a timeless lesson on spiritual mentoring and guidance through the ever-fresh word of Allah ﷻ, the Qur'an.

Muhammad, the Messenger of Allah ﷺ, was a magnificent soul and practiced much more than what he taught. No one was superior to Him in worship. He was given prophethood with a scripture, the Qur'an. His status was unique and incomparable. However, he ascended to the Heavenly realms by way of his servanthood. In other words, his servanthood came first, an introduction to his prophethood. In fact, this is the way the Qur'an commands him:

وَاعْبُدْ رَبَّكَ حَتّٰى يَأْتِيَكَ الْيَقِينُ

And (continue to) worship your Lord until what is certain [death] comes to you. (al-Hijr 15:99)

He obeyed the command of the Qur'an during his life and did not stop observing the requirements of servanthood to Allah ﷻ for an instant. That is why everything he said was welcomed and accepted in the general public's conscience. He told what he lived. He was saying and asking the things he had already fulfilled at the highest level. To give an example, his blessed wife, the mother of the believers, Aisha, narrated that the Prophet asked her one night, "O Aisha, will you allow me to be with my Lord tonight?" Aisha replied: "O Allah's Messenger! I like to be with you, but I like what you like more." Upon this, Aisha said that "the Prophet performed ablution and started the prayer. That night, he shed tears till morning and offered prayer."[68]

He was indeed a Prophet, a preacher, and a spiritual mentor and guide. And the most profound side of him was the unreachable depths of his servanthood. He wanted to continue the worship he had begun years before in the same way even during the last days of his life, when he was sick and in pain. However, during the last days, he could hardly move. He had suffered immensely throughout his life. He had experienced many specific problems related to his household and extended family. Moreover, his entire *ummah*'s worries pertaining to this world and the next were on his shoulders. He was certainly physically exhausted because of all these worries. After all, none other than him could have endured, even for a single day, what he suffered over his entire life.

Despite all this, he did not want to give up even the supererogatory worships he had previously started. These were such prayers that even one *rak'ah* (a unit of the daily prayers) would sometimes last hours. As he had no strength to stand up, he would offer them sitting, but he did not give them up.[69] He was an example of seriousness and fidelity that would last until the "hour" that is certain—in other words, until death, until Judgment Day, until eternity.

An important aspect of the spiritual guidance is this adherence and closeness to Allah ﷻ. After all, without this adherence and closeness, the person always hangs in midair, lives in the void. Once a person steps into the void, he or she remains alone with their own whims and desires.

The Prophet (pbuh) combined being close to Allah ﷻ with spiritual guidance in the best way possible. He was as deep, faultless, and perfect in his worship of and servitude to Allah ﷻ as he was as when he conveyed the message and guided others to the truth. Many times, when he began to offer his personal and extra prayers (*salat*), those who witnessed or joined him would think it would never come to an end. So were his prayers and supplications. When he raised his hands in prayer and supplication, people had the impression as if the hands would never come down again.

Once, the Companion Abdullah ibn Mas'ud joined one of the supererogatory night prayers (*tahajjud*) the Prophet offered. Abdullah had immediately started the prayer in order to benefit from the blessings of the prayer the Messenger of Allah ﷺ was offering. Abdullah narrated that the Messenger of Allah ﷺ was continuously reciting. He finished reciting Surah al-Baqarah. Abdullah thought he would bow down, but the Prophet ﷺ started to recite Surah Al 'Imran. He finished it, and Abdullah thought again that he would bow, but the Prophet ﷺ moved on to Surah an-Nisa and then Surah al-Maeda. He recited these four Surahs in the first *rak'ah*. Then, Abdullah said "an ill-thought" came to his mind for an instant. Those listening to Abdullah asked him: "*What was the ill-thought?*" He answered: "*It was to sit down and leave the Prophet [standing].*"[70]

As we see, the Messenger of Allah ﷺ told people about servanthood and practiced this servanthood himself at a level higher and more advanced than anyone else. He was so superior in this matter that even a leading Companion such as Abdullah ibn Mas'ud could not withstand the two-*rak'ah*-prayer he was offering.

In the period when the Prophet ﷺ was living his last moments, like a sun that was about to set, he put his head on his wife Aisha's knees and set his eyes on the heavens[71] (*al-mala' al-a'la*). He was quite weary but rather pre-occupied with the other-worldly Realms. He would faint from time to time, and when water was poured over his head and body, he would recover. As soon as he opened his eyes, the first thing he asked was: "*Have the people offered the prayer?*"[72]

The Prophet ﷺ always taught about the prayer, even on his deathbed. So did his community: they always lived in full consideration of the prayer. He was an exemplary man in every way, a perfect imam in every aspect, a magnificent leader, a just and enduring head of state!

Regarding the duty of spiritual guidance, one shouldn't overlook Allah's Messenger's ﷺ modest way of living and his togetherness with his Companions in all matters. When it was a matter of building a masjid, he carried bricks just as everybody else did; when it was a matter of digging a ditch, he broke a rock with a lever in his hand; and he always rushed to help his friends.[73] He taught others to be an ordinary person amongst the people and truly practiced it himself, too. When he invited people to austerity and asceticism, he would try to do the best in this matter. There would be times when for months no fire was lit to cook food in his house[74]; there was no mattress for him to sleep on.[75]

He was more meticulous and cautious than anyone else towards the unlawful, too. Once when his grandchild Hasan put one of the dates given as *sadaqah* (alms) in his mouth, the Prophet ﷺ got very scared; he immediately ran and took it out of the boy's mouth.[76] Hasan was a five or six-year-old boy at that time, but *sadaqah* was forbidden (*haram*) for both the Messenger of Allah ﷺ and his descendants.

One night, like so many nights, the Prophet ﷺ had not been able to sleep until the morning. He wept and prayed in pain. His wife Aisha asked in the morning what happened. The Messenger of Allah ﷺ answered: "*I found a date under my side [in the room], I took it, and I ate it. So I was afraid that it could be one of the dates of charity (sadaqah). That was the reason for my suffering.*"[77] However, that date was probably one of his personal dates since he used to put dates of charity in a separate place.

This sensitivity or caution is an outstanding example in terms of the qualities a true believer and a perfect spiritual mentor should possess.

f) Prayer

The Messenger of Allah ﷺ told his Companions and his entire *ummah* to identify, internalize and become integrated with prayer. He drew their attention to and warned them with the following Qur'anic verse:

قُلْ مَا يَعْبَؤُا بِكُمْ رَبِّي لَوْلَا دُعَاؤُكُمْ

Say: "My Lord would not care for you were it not for your prayer." (al-Furqan 25:77)

The Prophet ﷺ said prayers on every occasion during any day: he prayed before sleeping, after getting up, while eating or drinking, before and after entering the bathroom, while performing ablution, while putting on clothes, etc. It is impossible to find another person in the world who was, or is, so integrated with prayer. There is no other person who remembers Allah ﷻ, takes refuge in Him, and looks for His consent and approval in every step he takes.

It is this unique and exemplary life that has led so many Muslims to follow his example. His entire life—from his eating and drinking to his way of dressing, from the way he spoke to his manners and style of address, from his social and political attitudes to his diplomatic etiquette and practices—were all recorded in the social consciousness and public memory as if every instance of his life was being filmed. It was thanks to this magnificent life that Muslim societies have continued their existence.

Every moment of the sublime life of the Messenger of Allah ﷺ was related to the Almighty ﷻ, with no single frame left out. Every act of his, from daily worship to basic human needs, like eating, drinking, and sleeping, were all carried out in consciousness of the Divine and in relation to His approval and pleasure. It was for this reason that all his words and actions were firmly adopted by his Companions. They lived their faith with the utmost care, for it was what they saw in the example of their spiritual mentor, the Messenger of Allah ﷺ.

يَا اَيُّهَا الَّذِينَ اٰمَنُوا اتَّقُوا اللّٰهَ حَقَّ تُقَاتِهِ

O you who believe! Keep from disobedience to Allah in reverent piety, with all the reverence that is due to Him...

When this verse was revealed, the Companions asked, "How would it be possible to fear Allah ﷻ in accordance with His Majesty?" Out of concern that they would not be able to live up to this standard, they started abandoning all worldly pleasures, even food. The verse continued:

وَلَا تَمُوتُنَّ اِلَّا وَاَنْتُمْ مُسْلِمُونَ

... and see that you do not die save as Muslims (submitted to Him exclusively). (Al 'Imran 3:102)

This meant that without due fear of Allah ﷻ it would not be possible to die as a true believer. As such, none from the Companions went out to the market to carry out their business or commerce. Only at prayer times did they go to the masjid, and afterwards they confined themselves to their homes, continuously worshipping and praying. After several days, they had all lost weight, many almost starving. The Messenger of Allah ﷺ was aware of this situation, but he did not know the reason for this sudden change in them, as they had not shared their concerns with Him. They were afraid of opposing the Divine order. Later, another verse came to their rescue, teaching them that they were expected to show reverence "as much as" they could (at-Tagabun 64:16), after which the Companions were somewhat relieved.[78]

This is how the Companions were: sensitive, meticulous, and attentive regarding the Divine Revelation and putting them into practice in their lives. They were like this because their leader and guide, the Messenger, was like this, too. In fact, we could claim that the generations of Muslims that came over the next two or three centuries approached the Divine revelation with a similar attentiveness.

We have to keep this in mind: the duty of "calling to good and preventing evil" cannot be properly fulfilled unless Islam is understood and practiced with the same sensitivity as that of the Companions of the Prophet, who observed their faith to the minutest detail and made it their entire lives. Compared to other duties, "conveying the message" requires the guide to practice even more what he or she teaches—it cannot be theoretical only. "Living" the faith and "teaching" the faith are not mutually exclusive. It must be lived first and then explained. It should not be built on imaginary ideas or visions. Moreover, the luminous personalities who have shed light on us with their lives for centuries have always acted in this way: they themselves lived and practiced first what they were to teach. Thus, Allah ﷻ has made them successful because of their sincerity and truthfulness. So, if we want to be successful just like them, the only thing we must do is to follow in their footsteps. This is not far-fetched. Let me illustrate the argument with a few authentic examples from the Age of Happiness.

Umar ibn al-Khattab was a unique personality. After he was cruelly stabbed, he was lying on his deathbed in a coma. When he was asked if he wanted any food or drink, he did not have the strength even to say "no"; he could only move his eyes to indicate that he could not. But when somebody whispered in his ear "Umar! It is time for prayer," Umar, the comatose person, would suddenly sit up and confirm that he would pray. This is what he had seen in the example of the Prophet, peace be upon him. That great man, the caliph Umar, was stabbed during his prayer, and he would give his last breaths as he called for prayer.[79]

Another example in this issue is from the mother of believers, Aisha. One day, the Prophet found her crying. When he asked her why she was crying, she said: "*I thought about Hell.*"[80] That was how she saw the Prophet every night. The Messenger of Allah ﷺ nurtured her to develop such a consciousness with guidance through his own practice.

Their sensitivity, care, attentiveness, and sincerity were not only about the prayer or encouraging others to pray as well. They showed the same care to other principles of faith, too. Each of them was a spiritual guide like the Messenger of Allah ﷺ. For our mentoring and guidance to be effective, we need to live our faith as carefully as the Messenger ﷺ did.

The task and burden of conveying the message should never lead us to laxity in other deeds. It cannot be an excuse or reason for us to neglect other religious obligations. On the contrary, it must whip up our enthusiasm. We ourselves should practice what we are teaching much more enthusiastically than we expect from others. Any other attitudes, manners, and behaviors—and any words that do not confirm and verify one's own deeds—are all an expression of deception and a destruction of one's own credit.

When we look at the Messenger of Allah ﷺ, we see that he showed no negligence in practicing religion although he had so many pursuits and engagements. From establishing a great state in a short time—only twenty-three years—to his being closely concerned with all members of his *ummah*, and from dealing with domestic and foreign enemies to personally dealing with the problems of his household and extended family, there was no decrease, disruption, or negligence in his religious obligations and worship. Moreover, Allah ﷻ wanted him to ask for forgiveness and to pray more in return for the conquests and victories—and indeed, he always acted in accordance with the command of his Lord.[81]

Abu Bakr intensely and painfully struggled against events of collective rebellion and apostasy, but he would never give up his Night Prayers (*tahajjud*). He never neglected reciting the Qur'an in tears.

Umar defeated and stopped the aggression of the Byzantine Empire and the Sassanids, but he never stopped defeating his ego, either.[82]

While Uthman was dealing with all kinds of political sedition, he never gave up the supererogatory fasts and reading the Qur'an, even on the day he was martyred. His blood dripped on the leaves of the copy of the Qur'an in his hands, to be sealed for eternity. It is told that the verse on which the blood dripped was "*Allah is sufficient for you.*"[83]

Ali was acknowledged as "the Lion of Allah" on battlefields. His appellation was Haydar al-Karrar, which means a lion fighting over and over again. But he spent his nights in prostration. When he heard the *adhan* (call to prayer), he would fully concentrate and grow into an elevated spiritual state. And all these people would perform the duty of spiritual guidance without interruption.

The person who does the duty of mentoring and guidance must be serious and sincere with regards to doing what he or she says. This person may be a sheikh in a dervish lodge, an imam or preacher in a mosque, a teacher in a school, a lecturer in a university, a worker in a factory, or a student in a school. No matter what age they are and what profession they pursue, they must be serious and sincere in doing what they teach. Everyone should fulfill this responsibility according to their social status, depth of knowledge, and ability to assume responsibility—and they should perform this duty flawlessly.

While doing this duty, the sincerity and earnestness of the spiritual mentor is as important as what needs to be conveyed. The most evident sign showing the sincerity of the spiritual mentor is that he or she truly feels, deep within their conscience, the things they say and that they strive to live them in the best way they can. Guidance which is not associated with sincerity and practice—however successful it may seem—is shallow and inconsistent. It can hardly bring about any result; its effect, if any, is short-term and short-lived.

We should also keep in mind another aspect of conveying the message and living what one teaches. It is regarding the Hereafter and the punishment one incurs. The Messenger of Allah ﷺ describes a scene of the Hereafter regarding this matter as follows:

"During the night of my ascension, I passed by a group of people. Their lips were being severed with scissors of fire. I said, 'O Jibril (as)! Who are these people?' He said, "They are the preachers from your Ummah that would say other than what they would do."[84]

This is the situation of people who forget themselves and do not apply what they say while trying to guide others. What is needed today is people who live what they know and say, not those who just talk and argue. These are the people who will resolve the constraints and problems. Obstacles before our salvation can only be overcome by such people.

Those saddled with books or chatterboxes, talking day and night, can do nothing in terms of the people's deliverance. While the Ottoman Empire was collapsing, there were hundreds of thousands of books in the libraries. These books, however, could not prevent the fall and destruction of the empire. Books in those libraries are no different in quality from the load of information stored in a person's memory. What is essential is whether we act upon our knowledge or not.

The Messenger of Allah ﷺ points out this issue in a hadith as follows:

"What I fear most in my ummah is the hypocrisy of the scholars and the contention of the hypocrites."[85]

If the scholars act in a double-faced and double-tongued way, and if the hypocrites deceive people around them with eloquence, dialectics, and demagogy, this *ummah* is done for.

Spiritual mentors should perform in their own lives what they teach to others. This is our biggest shortcoming, which we often fail to notice as both individuals and institutions.

2.8. Inner purity and sincerity

While providing any civic service or spiritual mentoring, it is essential for the mentor to have, preserve, and maintain their purity of heart, mind, and intention. Any changes in social, political, and financial status, ranks, conditions, resources, and opportunities should not alter the mentor's initial inner purity, humility, and sincerity. For ease of reference in the following arguments, we will simply use the term for all these as "preserving the inner state."

Humility and modesty are at the core and essence of Islam. Social relations that are not shaped by true faith are generally egocentric. The "I," or the ego of these people, always bears a hidden arrogance. In such relationships, humility is replaced by pride and self-aggrandizement, and modesty is replaced by arrogance, self-conceit, and egocentrism—seeing no one but oneself.

These kinds of ego-centric weak spots exist in the nature of every human being. Unless they are edified properly and unless every one of them is replaced by virtues, the human becomes riddled with holes in terms of their spiritual nature. I can definitely say that whoever nurtures pride and arrogance in him or herself can rise to any rank, position or office; they can be anything—but they can never be a spiritual mentor or guide. They are far from mentoring and guidance, and guidance and mentoring are quite far from them, too.

The spiritual mentor is the person who maintains his or her inner state and remains unspoiled at all times and under all circumstances, who does not lose self-control, vision, and direction after achievements, and who accomplishes the task they undertake with the same inner purity and humility as the day they started. Their life, which started on a quite modest basis, continues and terminates in the same modest way. Even if they changed the world, made worldwide revolutions, and if one day the stars in the sky were laid like a cobblestone under their feet, there would not be a slightest shift or decadence in their attitude and behavior.

What we need most today is spiritual mentors or guides possessing this quality. What we need is effective mentors who can guide the masses constructively, make their voices heeded respectfully, and have the aspirations and inspirations of their hearts be reflected peacefully around them.

The most outstanding aspect of a sincere and truehearted believer is their humility and modesty. They have a very simple life. Their house and surroundings reflect this simple, plain nature. They have taken this praiseworthy quality from the Qur'an and the matchless life of the Messenger of Allah ﷺ. For, the Messenger, the Master of mentors ﷺ, always behaved and lived this way. He always retained the humility from his first preaching Islam in Mecca. He was equally humble on the day he entered Mecca, from which he had been compelled to leave eight years earlier. Although he was now the conqueror of the city with a large army, he bowed his head so low that his beard was touching his camel.[86] This was evidence as to how he had deepened his humility day after day.

One day, he was thirsty and asked for water. One of the Companions wanted to fetch clean water from a nearby home instead of the well in which everybody was putting their hands. The Messenger of Allah ﷺ stopped him and said that he wanted to drink water from the well.[87] He never wanted to have a privilege. He spent his entire life on a mat made of date palm leaves.[88] He departed from this world to the next on that mat; they lifted the mat he had slept on and buried him under it. That very spot, his Rawda, is more sacred to us than Paradise. So, there was no veering, no zigzagging, in his life; the way of spiritual guidance also must be so, I think.

When Umar was the caliph, he was ruling a very large country. Despite this, he, too, never changed the lifestyle he adopted after he embraced Islam. He was the poorest man of Medina when he became the caliph; he was the poorest when he died. It was reported that his garment had more than thirty patches.[89] Those who looked for him would generally find him in the cemetery of al-Baqi' in Medina, in deep contemplation. That was the unchanging lifestyle of the great caliph who had throned and dethroned kings! His natural state-of-being had the biggest effect on others as a great example.

Hatim al-Asam was one of the great imams and scholars of the science of Hadith. He heard that Muhammad ibn Muqatil, who was also a great scholar of the Hadith and Tafsir (Qur'anic Exegesis), was ill. Upon the suggestion of one of his friends, Hatim decided to pay him a visit. He went to the house of Ibn Muqatil together with his friend. But this was not an ordinary house; it was rather an impressive mansion, almost like a small palace. In the first place, Hatim hesitated to enter the mansion. Yet, he could not resist his friend's insistence and so entered. However, Hatim regretted doing so since the interior part of the house was more stately and pompous than its outside.

Ibn Muqatil was lying on his bed in his wonderful bedroom and a servant standing was continuously fanning to make him feel cool. Hatim, who was previously surprised, was shocked now. Ibn Muqatil was not an ordinary man; he was an important scholar. He was a man of devotion and prayer; he would rise to pray late at night and shed tears out of reverence to Allah ﷻ. Hatim thought that Ibn Muqatil, too, was in need of guidance in relation to what looked like his weakness for comfort and luxury. Hatim was a qualified person who could perform this duty. He wanted to do so and started by asking a question: "Through which chains of narrators do the hadiths you teach reach you?"

Ibn Muqatil thought this was an ordinary question of the Hadith Methodology and answered: "*All the narrators I teach from are 'reliable' (sika) people. For example, I narrate from so and so. This is a trustworthy person.*" He added, "*My master, my sheikh, is so and so forth.*"

Hatim: "*Who is your sheikh's sheikh? Who does he narrate from?*"

Ibn Muqatil: "*He narrates from so and so.*"

Hatim: "*Who does he narrate from?*"

Ibn Muqatil: "*From Ali ibn Abu Talib.*"

Hatim: "*Who does he narrate from?*"

Ibn Muqatil: "*From our Prophet (pbuh).*"

Hatim: "*Who does our Prophet narrate from?*"

Ibn Muqatil: "*Naturally from the Archangel Jibreel.*"

Hatim: "*Who does he narrate from?*"

Ibn Muqatil: "*From our Lord Almighty certainly.*"

Hatim made a witty retort here and said: "*This means that hadiths reach you through so reliable chains of narrators. Can you tell me now whether any one of hadiths reaching you includes a narration about the virtues of living in such a mansion, among such servants and in such a cozy bed?*"

The more Hatim spoke, the more Ibn Mukatil went all shades of red and became deeply embarrassed. His illness was suddenly aggravated. People around him interfered and said to Hatim, "*Stop talking, you will kill the man.*" However, Hatim replied in a more severe way: "*It is you who kill him by acting like this and treating him in this way.*"[90]

To keep quiet, to remain silent, in the face of those who set out for spiritual mentoring and guidance but later changed their lifestyle because of the favor people show them is indeed to harm them, is indeed to kill them. Hatim al-Asam had done the best thing that had to be done at that moment.

On a different occasion, Hatim paid a visit to Imam al-Tanafisi, who was among the great scholars of his era. Since he had close contact with the state officials, his standard of living was at a level that can be called luxurious. Hatim said to him: "*Sir, would you check my performing the ablution and correct me if I make a mistake?*" An ewer and basin were brought and Hatim started washing himself. However, when washing his face, he washed it four times instead of three. Al-Tanafisi immediately interrupted him: "*You will wash it three times. The fourth is squandering.*"

Those words were exactly what Hatim already expected to hear. He stopped performing the ablution and said: "*You say washing my face one more time, my using a handful of water more, is squandering. Isn't it squandering spending your entire life in this palace, in this pomp and magnificence, on these carpets? Or did Islam forbid us squandering only for ablution?*"[91]

Tanafisi, too, was a great scholar and a virtuous person. However, his close contact with state officials had pulled him to such an understanding of life. As this way of living does not suit the lifestyle of a true spiritual guide, Hatim had decided to warn and guide him as well.

Those who live such a luxurious life today are unfortunately slipping to this lethal ground generally due to a mistaken consideration. They are not aware of it themselves, but it seems they could not discover their true essence and want to make up for the deficiencies in their character by living in luxury, which arises from an inferiority complex. A person with integrity in their character would not go for such lowly things, like chasing a luxurious life.

Humility is a sign of greatness. When one learns to be an ordinary person, one learns how to be a true human being. Those who grow with accidental causes or external sources are susceptible to be nothing when these causes or sources disappear. If it is wealth, property, rank, or office that gives a person greatness, when they are lost or taken away, it means a total collapse or devastation for that person. However, a person's value, their self-worth, should come from their inner self and state, from their intrinsic essence, so that incidental things and conditions do not cause any harm in them, so that they always remain as themselves. Casual impacts cannot erode a person who is his or her true self.

Even death and departing from this life cannot finish them. The hearts of hundreds of thousands of people will be an eternal abode for them. No matter if such individuals have no house or a residence of their own in this world, and no matter if they lead a life on a mat, in humility and modesty, without any luxury or comfort, no matter if there isn't even a tombstone marking their burial site… He or she will be a much sought-after, admired, and visited here in this world and the beyond.

In brief, spiritual mentors or guides should live a plain, pure, simple life. Whatever the point, level, rank or status they eventually reach and attain in social life, they must pay attention not to spoil and tarnish this plainness, purity, humility, and sincerity.

2. 9. Relationship with authorities and the elite

With the exception of when their spiritual mentoring duty requires them to do so, a spiritual mentor or guide should not be in very close association with state officials, civil authorities, and the rich and wealthy elite who wield political power. If he or she needs to provide them with guidance they may do so by staying clear of any political and financial motives, pursuits, incentives, or interests. In hadith collections, it is reported that the worst of the learned are those who frequently visit the rulers or state authorities, while the most beneficial of the rulers or state authorities are those who frequently visit the learned.[92]

Spiritual guides should not be indebted to anyone for anything. They should not owe anyone a favor or a debt of gratitude, in order to prevent any potential conflicts of interest that may compromise their values, character, and credibility. Those who become slaves to their stomach at the banquets or who knock on the doors of officials frequently to fawn over them can have no influence on the officials nor on any other person. This is due to the inherent reality that we as humans are always indebted to the favors made to us. On the other hand, if the rich and state officials visit the spiritual mentors—provided that there is no exploitation or ulterior motives—this would be an admirable act on their behalf. Only in this way can the true spiritual mentor provide appropriate guidance and help them benefit from their spiritual teaching. This would certainly serve as a breath of fresh air, especially for those who grow depressed due to the stresses of social, commercial, and administrative life.

When Umar ibn Abd al-Aziz[20] was the caliph, he always had a group of learned men by his side. Although Umar was living a more ascetic life than they did, he would never neglect consulting with them. Raja' ibn Haywah[21] was one of them. There were others, and Umar went to their feet to listen to their discussions and lessons. Ubaydullah ibn Abdullah, a

20 Umar ibn Abd al-Aziz (682-720), or Umar II, was the eighth Umayyad caliph. He is known to be a Reviver (mujaddid) and his name is usually included among the Rightly Guided Caliphs.

21 Raja Ibn Haywah al-Kindi was a leading Islamic jurist, adviser, and Arabic calligraphist, who is also best known as the likely artist responsible for the detailed inscriptions on the Dome of the Rock in Jerusalem, which was completed in 692.

hadith narrator and jurist, was another teacher Umar visited. Umar would say about him: "*I'd deem an hour spent near Ubaydullah worth a lifetime.*" He would always listen to the words of the luminaries with great attention and try to learn from the assemblies of conversation as much as possible. Yet, Umar ibn Abd al-Aziz was as erudite as those he would listen to. This is the defining characteristic that made him Umar ibn Abd al-Aziz. For this reason, although he served as the caliph for almost two and a half years, his achievements were worth as much as fifty years of service.

Contrarily, there have been others who claimed to have frequented state authorities to preach to them, but who, later, did not only fail to guide them but also lost all their spiritual gifts, and they themselves went down the wrong path. Frequently visiting people of status and wealth is not the way of the Messenger of Allah ﷺ. This must be done when necessary, but the distance should be maintained in a such a way that does not compromise the real purpose of spiritual guidance.

Even during the Meccan era, the dignitaries of the Quraysh asked the Messenger of Allah ﷺ to devote a day especially to them. On such a day, they asked the Prophet to sit with them on his own and not to bring his Companions, such as Bilal, Ammar, Suhayb, Khabbab, and Ibn Mas`ud, with him. They demanded he exclude the Companions, as they regarded them as not among the Meccan elites. A revelation immediately came and what they had asked was strictly forbidden[93]:

وَاصْبِرْ نَفْسَكَ مَعَ الَّذِينَ يَدْعُونَ رَبَّهُمْ بِالْغَدٰوةِ وَالْعَشِيِّ يُرِيدُونَ وَجْهَهُ وَلَا تَعْدُ عَيْنَاكَ
عَنْهُمْ تُرِيدُ زِينَةَ الْحَيٰوةِ الدُّنْيَا وَلَا تُطِعْ مَنْ اَغْفَلْنَا قَلْبَهُ عَنْ ذِكْرِنَا وَاتَّبَعَ هَوٰيهُ
وَكَانَ اَمْرُهُ فُرُطًا

And keep yourself patient, along with those who invoke their Lord morning and evening, seeking His "Face" (His eternal, good pleasure, and the meeting with Him in the Hereafter); and do not let your eyes pass beyond them, desiring the beauties of the life of this world (by the participation of those of leading positions among people in your assemblies). And pay no heed to (the desires of) him whose heart We have made unmindful of Our remembrance, who follows his lusts and fancies, and whose affair exceeds all bounds (of right and decency). (al-Kahf 18:28)

The Messenger's high, noble, righteous spirit would never even consider accepting such a proposal. Moreover, Allah ﷻ commanded the Prophet to patiently content himself with sitting with those Companions who called on their Lord morning and afternoon. "Patience" implies that he should continue to be the way he was. Therefore, Allah ﷻ told our Prophet that the state he was in was positive and satisfactory, and that he must continue in this manner. As a matter of fact, the Messenger of Allah ﷺ never had any tendency to accept the proposal of the polytheists of Mecca.

In sum, our Prophet ﷺ was a mentor and guide, and the Qur'an is the Book teaching us methods and principles exemplified in the character of the most perfect mentor, peace be upon him. One of the principles taught by the Qur'an is to keep distance from people of wealth and status, the rich, and the elite governing bodies and not to owe any favors to them, so that mentors may continue their guidance without compromising the independence of their soul. There is much to gain if religious mentors like this can be nurtured. However, as long as the masses remain deluded by the so-called mentors whose souls are rife with collusion and materialism, we will still be waiting for the true mentors and guides for years to come and to call people to good and preventing wrong.

2. 10. Being resolute

Being resolute is one of the most admirable attributes of a mentor or guide and indicates their faithfulness, purposefulness, and steadfastness in fulfilling the duty of calling to good and preventing wrong. It implies determination and consistency in carrying out the duty of mentoring and guiding people to individual and collective good.

Resoluteness in adherence to Allah ﷻ, in conveying the message, and guiding others to the bliss here and in the beyond is the surest way of gaining Allah's ﷻ approval. It is also the sign of the mentor's sincerity and the secret of making what is conveyed reflect in the conscience of the people addressed.

Resoluteness in doing something is the most evident sign that the matter is dealt with carefully and responsibly in accordance with its importance. We know that Allah ﷻ highly regards a person giving his or her testimony of faith—that there is none worthy of worship except Allah ﷻ and Muhammad is His servant and Messenger ﷺ. Allah wants this testimony to have its due place in the heart of human beings. Since the spiritual mentors devote themselves to what Allah ﷻ attaches importance to and since they do their best to make His message take root in hearts and minds, they will naturally have responded in the same way to the things Allah ﷻ deems important. This is what we mean by being "resolute" in this section.

In addition, respecting, holding in high honor, observing the sanctity of the symbols and rites of Allah ﷻ, and acknowledging as important what He praises is a sign of piety and reverence to Him in one's heart. The Qur'an says:

ذٰلِكَ وَمَنْ يُعَظِّمْ شَعَائِرَ اللّٰهِ فَإِنَّهَا مِنْ تَقْوَى الْقُلُوبِ

That (is the truth itself). And whoever venerates the rites (public symbols and rituals) set up by Allah, surely it is because of the true piety and the consciousness of Allah of their hearts. (al-Hajj 22:32)

The Messenger of Allah ﷺ, too, held in high honor the testimony of the oneness of Allah ﷻ (*kalima tawheed*) in a hadith as, "*Whoever says la ilaha illallah truly from his heart, then he will enter paradise.*"[94] The Prophet ﷺ always exalted and inculcated this in his Companions. An incident related to the Companion Khalid ibn Walid is timely here. The Prophet ﷺ had honored Khalid ibn Walid with the title of "The Sword of Allah." Thus, this was as if the Prophet ﷺ had congratulated Khalid on his prospective victories and conquests from the beginning.

During a battle, Khalid killed someone who said "La ilaha illallah" at the last moment. The Messenger of Allah ﷺ became very sad because of Khalid's action. He raised his hands and supplicated to Allah ﷻ, saying twice, "*O Allah! I am free from what Khalid has done.*"[95]

Let me say again: the spiritual mentor respects and holds in high honor, and acknowledges as important, what Allah ﷻ praises and deems important. This shows how sincere and devoted the mentor is for the duty. They perform the duty with no expectation of reward or personal gain in return. Those who are not resolute in this way and who do not devote their lives to this duty cannot be a spiritual mentor or guide. It would also be wrong to call one a "spiritual mentor" if they are not resolute.

The spiritual mentor should explain the matters again and again in a tireless way, if need be. He or she should wait for the right time and the right place to teach others. Then they try to seize the right moment when their interlocutor is ready to accept the message. They will continue teaching for a lifetime without being hurt and offended, just as all the

Prophets have done. The Prophets' lives were totally resolute, consistent, and unwavering, and they conveyed the truth steadfastly.

After he had been honored with the Prophethood, the Prophet taught Islam incessantly for twenty-three years, always with this resoluteness. He went many times to Abu Jahl, the staunch opposer of the truth, and told him about Islam. He organized and gave countless banquets for the notables of Mecca and tried to communicate the message during such events.[96]

The Companions were of the same consciousness and enthusiasm, too. Resoluteness was an inseparable quality of theirs. Likewise, all the great people who succeeded the Companions adopted the same resoluteness, steadfastness, and unswerving faithfulness.

Resoluteness is a natural consequence of the person knowing about their duty and realizing what they are supposed to do in the name of mentoring and guidance. Every spiritual guide should know very well that their duty is *only* to convey and explain, so that they do not interfere and disrespect Divine Will and that they do not do any injustice towards the interlocutors they address. Making people find the true faith and attain guidance is neither a task for the mentors alone, nor is it their duty. That duty belongs to Allah ﷻ. Yet, whether or not the interlocutor embraces the faith, the mentor who has conveyed the message obtains Allah's ﷻ reward for it. Moreover, the mentor thinking and acting in this way is like a secret code of acceptance of the truths they conveyed. Expecting the result from Allah ﷻ alone is a sign of sincerity or purity of intention, which is the essence and source of all worship.

2.11. Being insightful and conforming with innate human nature

The spiritual mentor must never be in conflict with the laws decreed by innate human nature and should act with insight. One's inner nature has its roots in the laws of creation. Acting with insight requires one to present his or her ideas to people in accordance with these laws. In other words, certain inherent qualities of character should be taken into account and what is said should be said accordingly. Otherwise, no matter how brilliant, how attractive, the words are, they may not be welcomed and accepted by the interlocutor, because he or she may not understand them at all or may find them fantastical or utopian.

Let me explain it with a few human feelings or emotions ingrained in human nature, like love and affection, determination and stubbornness, yearning for immortality and eternity, the desire to acquire status, rank, recognition, and office, and a few more.

Every human being has the feeling of love or affection. It would be wrong to ignore this feeling and react to it as if it did not exist at all. People should not be told not to love. It would be in vain, no use at all, and such a demand does not comply with reality. What a spiritual mentor can do, then, is to help the interlocutor to channel the potential love in him or her to the eternal and everlasting love, instead of being just infatuated and consumed with the worldly, finite, temporal, and ephemeral forms. If this feeling of love is devoted and exhausted only to the mortal and the transient, it turns out to be an ordeal. If it is directed towards Allah ﷻ, it can be a means for the person to rise spiritually. Therefore, instead of telling people not to love, it would be right to ask people to "love the Ever-Lasting and Infinite Beloved, and everything else for the sake of Him." Loving all creation for the sake of Him would not be inappropriate, as the poet Yunus Emre put it: "*Love creatures for the sake of—because of—the Creator.*"

Every person possesses the feeling of stubbornness, which sometimes causes conflict and brings out a person's worst qualities. What lies beneath conflicts and disputes today is evidently stubbornness. There is rage and violence where this feeling prevails. There is balance and moderation where people can control it. This feeling, which has many negative aspects on the surface, was given to humans for a certain purpose and wisdom. For example, stubbornness is a very important part of being steadfast in the way of truth. If there was no feeling of stubbornness, everybody who faced a little pressure would turn away from the truth. This means that it is possible to obtain very good results if we channel this feeling in a positive direction. Therefore, it is more useful to tell people to transform their stubbornness into determination, to show perseverance in the way of the truth, instead of telling them simply to give up obstinacy.

Furthermore, humans have a yearning for immortality and eternity. However, they are not eternal—their biological nature cannot last forever. They have a beginning and an end. Life, which begins with the meeting of the sperm and the egg in the mother's womb, starts giving signals of death as soon as it begins. Despite all these, humans can't eradicate their yearning for eternity. In fact, that feeling is given to them for a higher goal, which is to gain eternal life. Therefore, human beings must use this feeling given to them properly—that is, to transform it, to desire an eternal life in Paradise and to attain the pleasure of Allah's ﷻ eternal beauty and perfection. Otherwise, this feeling will be a whip of torment that will always remind humans of their helplessness and nothingness. A person continuously suffering under this whip can neither have integrity nor find inner peace.

Similarly, humans have a desire for position and status. Rising non-stop and climbing or jumping to the peak of one's goal are among the irrepressible weaknesses of many people. Therefore, the spiritual mentor must discern this feeling in the interlocutors and show them why this feeling was given to them. The desire to rise in status was given to humans in order to encourage them to "rise to the highest ranks in Paradise" and to the highest degree of virtues in this world. However, discerning and discovering these feelings and using their power for the benefit of the interlocutor depend on the perception and insight of the spiritual mentor.

Spiritual mentoring and guiding are not always rosy. There may be obstacles, trials, and tribulations, as well as agony and pain, along this road. Distractions, adversity, and challenges may obstruct mentors and guides because there have always been ideological and interest groups opposing spiritual mentoring and guidance. Therefore, the spiritual mentor and guide must accept at the very outset that there might be hardships and suffering along this blessed path. The experiences of the Prophets, saints, martyrs, and all pious spiritual teachers confirm this. This is the destiny of the path of mentoring and guidance. Supporters of this blessed task of calling to good and preventing wrong may not be totally free from what the preceding holy people were subjected to. This is, as it were, a natural direction for mentors to go. Deviating from this direction due to likely hardships and pain means deviating from the sine non qua of human existence and collective benevolence. Those who give up or deviate from this duty can no longer be called a spiritual mentor or guide.

Prophet Nuh suffered this ordeal for centuries. Prophet Ibrahim was excommunicated and thrown into the fire because he was trying to fulfill this duty. Prophet Musa suffered in ancient Egypt and the Sinai Peninsula. Prophet Yahya (John) was cut into two; the Isa Messiah was subjected to betrayal and persecution and did not ever have a comfortable life. It is a very heavy duty and requires unshakeable willpower. Those who cannot love this fate, who cannot endure its trials and tribulations with their own choice and free will, cannot follow in the footsteps of the Prophets. If they happen to start in some way, their willpower eventually weakens and fails, and then they come undone, their knees give away, and they fall…

Let me share an incident from the early period of Islam: Harith ibn Harith told a story about how, when as a child, he was going to the Ka'ba with his father. They saw a group swarming a person in their midst. His father thought he was a Sabean. He later realized he was the Prophet ﷺ, who was continuously saying, "O people, say *la ilaha illallah* and be saved." At that moment, his daughter Zainab came running there crying and started wiping the traces of blood from her father's face. The Messenger of Allah ﷺ consoled his daughter and said, *"O daughter, do not fear for your father."*[97]

This kind of events engraved in the childhood memory of Harith ibn Harith was a part of many Muslims' everyday lives, and especially of Allah's Messenger's ﷺ life, during the Meccan era.

Another day, the Messenger of Allah ﷺ was offering prayer in the Ka'ba. Uqba ibn Abi Mu'ait, the worst evildoer of his tribe, came from behind him and put his sheet round the Prophet's neck and squeezed it tightly to strangle the Messenger ﷺ. Abu Bakr came and pushed Uqba away from the Prophet and said, "Will you kill a man just because he says, 'My Lord is Allah?"[98]

Allah ﷻ knows how many times Abu Bakr himself had been beaten, fainted somewhere in Mecca's streets, and was dragged home by a few people who knew him. The first words of his when he opened his eyes were: *"How is the Messenger of Allah?"*[99]

The Companion Ammar, his father Yasir, and his mother Sumayya were made to wear coats of iron armor and left to swelter in the blistering sun. Yasir and Sumayya were engraved in history's memory as the first martyrs.[100] While Bilal al-Habashi was being crushed under boulders he uttered, "*Ahad, Ahad* (the One—Allah is the One)"; as he did so, he seemed to prove deserving of being the first *muezzin* (caller to prayer) of the Prophet.[101] Talha ibn Ubaydullah's hands and feet were tied as he dragged along the streets by his mother to denigrate him as an inferior.[102] Zubayr ibn al-Awwam was wrapped in a burning straw mat until the smoke appeared—it was the fluid in his skin burning.[103] In fact, all those and more reflect the fate of this way.

Another striking example is related to the Companion Abdullah ibn Hudhafah as-Sahmi. Abdullah was captured by the Romans during the Caliphate of Umar. He was tortured for days and forced to convert to Christianity. When he refused to do so, they decided to execute him. He cried while walking towards the gallows. When he was asked the reason, Abdullah said he was not crying out of fear, but because he had only one life to give away for the sake of Allah ﷻ, and he wished he had a thousand.[104]

Another report narrates the same story somewhat differently: While Abdullah was walking towards the gallows with a smile on his face, a priest approached him and said, "*My son, you will be executed in a few minutes. I asked and was given permission to tell you at this moment about Christianity, the true religion. You will win everlasting life even if you lose your present life when executed. However, if you accept Christianity, this may please the Emperor and he may forgive you.*" Abdullah answered him in a serious and dignified way: "*Dear priest! I don't know how to thank you right now. I was very sorry about dying without telling anyone about the truth. Now you have given me this opportunity. If I can tell you about Islam, which is the true religion, in these few minutes, I won't be grieved even if I die. Because this will probably help you to save your eternal life!*" The priest and everyone present were thunderstruck by his words since none of them could fathom his desire to "convey the message."

The ardor and enthusiasm of the spiritual guide must always be like a sun that never sets. Illuminating the surroundings must become the purpose of his or her life. The way to success passes through hardships and suffering. When involuntary, compulsory endurance comes to an end, then voluntary, optional privation (the state of being deprived of or lacking an attribute formerly or properly possessed) starts. Let me illustrate this.

Allah's Messenger ﷺ observed his discretionary privation even when the public treasury was overflowing. Sometimes a week passed, and the Messenger ﷺ did not put a single morsel in his mouth. Abu Hurayrah narrates: "*One day I entered Allah's Messenger's room. I saw that he was offering the prayer while sitting. After the prayer, I asked him whether he was ill. He answered, 'No, Abu Hurayrah, I am not ill. But hunger (made me feeble).' I started to cry. He consoled me saying, 'Don't cry Abu Hurayrah! Those suffering of hunger in this world will not be subjected to severe torment on the Day of Judgment.*'"[105]

Ibn Abbas reported: "The Messenger of Allah ﷺ would spend several nights in a row with an empty stomach, and his family would not find anything for dinner. Most of their bread was made from barley."[106]

Islam, with all its magnificence, was established on the foundations of such a life. And if it is to prevail in hearts again, it will do so by rising on the shoulders of the people of faith and action possessing and representing the same spirit. This great task is not a desk job, so to speak, nor is it for masters of bureaucracy or carefree upstarts.

This universal truth can be seen in the advice Luqman (pbuh) gave to his son, and by implication, to the young who are the great representatives of spiritual guidance. The Qur'an confirms this advice as an eternal principle and presents it to us as such:

يَا بُنَيَّ اَقِمِ الصَّلٰوةَ وَأْمُرْ بِالْمَعْرُوفِ وَانْهَ عَنِ الْمُنْكَرِ وَاصْبِرْ عَلٰى مَا اَصَابَكَ
اِنَّ ذٰلِكَ مِنْ عَزْمِ الْاُمُورِ

"*My dear son! Establish prayer, encourage what is good and forbid what is evil, and endure patiently whatever befalls you. Surely this is a resolve to aspire to.*" *(Luqman 31:17)*

The verse expresses that the one observing prayer and calling people to good and preventing wrong will inevitably be subjected to trials and tribulations. These are the different aspects of the same truth here: 1) offering prayers; 2) calling to good and preventing wrong; and 3) enduring patiently in the face of hardships and troubles. The person who does one of these has achieved only one aspect of this truth; the one who does the two has achieved both aspects of it and is supposed to be on the right way to Allah ﷻ. As for the third, along with the other two, of course, it renders the person a true and complete human being and an ideal mentor or guide. Living and representing all of the three aspects is the path of the great ones. For this reason, those who are the candidates for shouldering the duty of the Prophets should be determined to go through the same way. What those who behave otherwise do is just an adventure. One should always take refuge in Allah ﷻ from being dragged to such adventures, as it is uncertain when, where, and on whose account, they will end or perish.

I already mentioned above that the basis of spiritual mentoring is to be in compliance with the laws of innate nature and also to act with insight. Besides, knowing the nature and disposition of the people who would take on the task are crucially important. The best example to us in this matter is again the Messenger of Allah ﷺ. One of the pieces of evidence to his Prophethood—which is closely relevant to our subject—is that he employed every human being in a service that suited their talents and was appropriate to their disposition. This in fact is a sign of his intelligence, perception, and sagacity. He was never in a situation where he had to regret because he assigned a certain person to a certain duty. This insight, foresight, and accuracy, which he showed throughout his life, is among the most important signs and pieces of evidence of his Prophethood.

For example, he chose the poet Hassan ibn Thabit to counter the verbal attacks of pagans. Hassan was victorious in all the duel of words he entered.[107] If Hassan had been employed in the battlefield and been given the position of commander in chief, this Companion, so successful in the battle of words, might have caused a crushing defeat in the battle of swords.

The Messenger ﷺ sent Companions such as Mus'ab ibn Umayr, Muadh ibn Jabal, Ali ibn Abu Talib, and some others to mentor and guide. And they used to obtain incredible successes in terms of conveying the message wherever they went. However, if the same task had been given to the commander Khalid ibn Walid, he probably would not have been able to do it to the same degree. He was created to scare the lion-hearted soldiers in the battlefield, and the Messenger of Allah ﷺ always assigned him to such positions.

Choosing the right individuals and assigning them appropriate tasks according to their inner and outer talents is among the most important aspects of a spiritual mentor. This, of course, depends on knowing human nature well. The successes of those who do not know the human being both with their weaknesses and merits are always disputable. Moreover, it is not possible to prevent the wasting of resources and people unless every single person is properly employed. The spiritual mentor is the one who handles and accomplishes this task with his or her insight. They manage to overcome and succeed in the heaviest tasks by acting in accordance with the laws of nature, and thus they reach successes beyond their own power and strength.

Chapter 3

The Spiritual Characteristics of a Mentor

This chapter will focus on the spiritual anatomy of a mentor. The hope is to make the path of mentors even brighter by highlighting some of their expected spiritual characteristics. The inner world of every human is unique; this is why some themes covered in this chapter might have nuances and different implications in the soul of every reader.

3.1. Compassion

The spiritual mentor must first and foremost be compassionate. He or she must be a hero of compassion. They must not make people accept the truth by compulsion or brute strength. It is never possible to make faith in Allah ﷻ prevail in one's heart by compulsion. In mentoring and guidance, compassion towards the interlocutors softens and melts their hearts to the reception of the truth. It facilitates and renders their hearts ready to accept Allah ﷻ and His Messenger ﷺ.

The mentor leads the interlocutor to the truth by convincing arguments. He or she molds the interlocutors' way of thinking with knowledge. His or her exemplary attributes and virtues nurture a liking for or interest in themselves and the message given. The fact that interlocutors see and acknowledge the mentor as an exemplary character equipped with virtues is obviously influential in the acceptance of what is conveyed. Individuals and groups are always concerned and frightened of those who present matters in a highhanded and despotic manner. Such a manner worries and scares people away even if what is conveyed is true. No matter how warm, appealing, or crucial a message, the cold or off-putting manner of the speaker will have a negative effect on the listeners. Such an attitude or behavior brings no benefit but only harm. No one has the right to alienate and frighten people from Islam because of their own mistakes.

The Messenger of Allah ﷺ was the exemplar of compassion as he was for all other virtues. He founded his great mission and duty on important fundamentals, and compassion was one of them. He invited others to his call in the warm atmosphere of compassion. He is reported to have said *"I am to you as a father is to his children."*[108] It is also told that no sooner than he was born, he miraculously said, *"My ummah."*[109] This is similar to a very affectionate father saying, "my child" and embracing him or her, the fruit of his heart. Prophet Yaqub (Jacob) had only Yusuf (Joseph) as his dear one, whereas every member of Prophet Muhammad's ﷺ own *ummah* was a Yusuf for him, peace be upon them.

He opened his bosom to each member of his *ummah* with the affection of a father to his child and every member of His *ummah* would love him more than their own parents, even more than their own beings. Therefore, behaviors that are reciprocated with affection and respect arising from compassion must be an irrevocable quality of the spiritual mentor. There is no love, affection, and respect where compassion does not exist. It is possible to make people obey something by force. However, it is not possible to make them love the truths you communicate to them in this way. There is no locked door that compassion cannot open. Ice that does not melt with compassion cannot be melted by anything else. If you want to connect people to one another with warm affection or love, you must first behave with compassion.

No individual and social problem can be solved satisfactorily unless you forgive people's mistakes and show them the truth with compassion. Our Prophet describes his attitude towards his *ummah*'s mistakes in the following way, with a representation and analogy:

إِنَّمَا مَثَلِي وَمَثَلُ النَّاسِ كَمَثَلِ رَجُلٍ اسْتَوْقَدَ نَارًا فَلَمَّا أَضَاءَتْ مَا حَوْلَهُ جَعَلَ الْفَرَاشُ
وَهَذِهِ الدَّوَابُّ الَّتِي تَقَعُ فِي النَّارِ يَقَعْنَ فِيهَا فَجَعَلَ يَنْزِعُهُنَّ وَيَغْلِبْنَهُ فَيَقْتَحِمْنَ
فِيهَا فَأَنَا آخُذُ بِحُجَزِكُمْ عَنْ النَّارِ وَهُمْ يَقْتَحِمُونَ فِيهَا

"My example and the example of the people is that of a man who made a fire, and when it lighted what was around it, moths and other insects started falling into the fire. The man tried (his best) to prevent them, (from falling in the fire) but they overpowered him and rushed into the fire. … Now, simi-

larly, I take hold of the knots at your waist (belts) to prevent you from falling into the Fire, but you insist on falling into it."[110]

Allah's Messenger ﷺ opens before us a broad avenue in terms of guidance. He reminds us that masses can embrace your message collectively on this road if we follow his direction. Pathways that digress from compassion will make the matter shallow and corrupt and lead some people to a serious loss.

If you can approach today's people with compassion, you will see that almost everybody has some sort of a broken, aggrieved heart. For nobody can be happy while sunken in sin. No one is staying in their unpleasant, undesirable situation willingly or voluntarily, except those whose consciences are totally blackened and whose spiritual worlds are completely decayed. They must have made a mistake and are unable to find a way to get out of it. Your helping hand of compassion will show them the way out they are truly seeking.

A person who is approached with compassion and balance—even if he or she does not accept your message at that very moment—will always regard you kindly and the matters you talk about positively. The fact that people who were most unlikely to embrace the truth opened to guidance and embraced faith at the most unexpected time is a reality that has thousands of examples. As those people are guided to the righteousness of faith by means of you, they will carry feelings of indebtedness and gratitude to you for the rest of their life. Moreover, a duplicate of all the good deeds they have done will be credited to you as well.

Let me give an example here to clarify the subject. Let us suppose that there is a fire and someone you do not like is in danger of burning along with all his family. Or let us suppose that a ship has sunken and people unfamiliar to you are in the sea waiting for a rescuing hand. You would immediately take action to save that person you do not like or those people you do not know, and you would even risk your life for theirs. You would not listen to anyone trying to dissuade you since the voice of your conscience would be more powerful or effective than any other voice at that moment. Rescuing these people from the fire or from being drowned is a point related to their worldly life—say, a life of fifty or sixty years. What, then, should our attitude towards those who are to be rescued in terms of their eternal life? The whole point is being able to comprehend this. Not reproaching people in that state for the things they do—let alone getting angry towards them—is an obligation for every person of conscience. While the whole humanity is suffering from material and spiritual disasters, afflicted with the plights concerning their present and the next world, spiritual mentors today should approach them with compassion. Anger, rage, compulsion, or violence of any sort do not befit a spiritual guide. Political interests and lies are not even close to them. Mentors exist as heroes of love and compassion, which the hearts in need of guidance and peace expect. And in this regard, Allah's Messenger ﷺ is our guiding light.

Look at his life! He had to endure so much just to guide people to Allah ﷻ. They stoned him, shed his blood, strangled him almost to death, put animal entrails on his head while praying, put thorns on the path he would cross... Allah's Messenger ﷺ always wanted people to embrace the truth. He always wanted even his enemies to reform and thus go to Paradise. He had no interest in his own name and expected no favor to himself from them.

When he had been stoned in Taif, he sought refuge in a vineyard. His body was covered in blood. Zayd was with him. An angel came down and asked the Messenger ﷺ for permission to destroy Taif: *"Order what you wish. If you like, I will let Al-Akh-Shabain* [i.e., two mountains surrounding Taif] *fall upon them."* The Prophet, the paragon of compassion, said, *"No. I hope that Allah will let them have children who will worship Allah and none besides Him."* [111] He did not wish any calamity to fall upon this town.

In the battlefield, his tooth was broken, and a piece of his helmet pierced his face. He immediately raised his hands to plead with His Lord to prevent the Divine wrath before his blood dropped to the ground. *"My Lord, forgive my people, because they have no knowledge [of me],"*[112] a prayer which is filled with compassion.

Here I would like to share the story of a young man who embraced the path of guidance after some years in disbelief. He now loves being among other faithful young people, so he frequently comes to their gatherings. At one such gathering, they talk about how the unfaithful anarchists have been wreaking havoc through violence. Hearing about this violence, one among them cannot control his feelings and says, "We must get rid of them!" The one who has recently embraced the true faith suddenly grows pale and says to his excited friend: "*Don't speak so, my friend. If you had made such a decision and got rid of them just a few days ago, I would not be here today. But as you see, today I am among you. Everybody needs the same soft friendship you showed to me. Otherwise, their eternal life will be lost, and this will do no good neither to us nor to them...*"

These words I have shared are as if told in the name of the whole youth suffering from disbelief. Like that young man, I would like to scream at the top of my voice that "all the young who are suffering from disbelief need your compassion." It is not possible to obtain anything by direct and violent actions. We have to act with our mind and reason, rather than with our feelings. What is essential is to convince people with arguments and guide them rationally to the world of the heart. A spiritual mentor should not even enter debates to silence people unless it is absolutely necessary.

Generations of young people have been lost or ruined without guidance. Desires have been obstacles on the paths leading to Allah ﷻ and His Grace and Mercy. Corporeal pleasures have been their ultimate goal. Nothing has been taught to them in the name of the truth, religion, faith, and the Qur'an. Not surprisingly, they are struggling desperately in a whirl. It is not those lost generations or the young we should be angry at. Those who really deserve disapproval and condemnation are the ones who pushed them to this misadventure. If there is a flaw, it is theirs. I do not claim that the young are totally innocent and blameless, but blaming them to their face in anger does no good in terms of rescuing them. We hope that the whole generation can get out of this whirl as soon as possible. This is our purpose and the ideal of existence. And we have no intention, consideration, or motives beyond that.

3.2. Selflessness

Selflessness, or self-sacrifice, refers to magnanimity of heart, embracing others with grace, and altruism in the sense of giving up one's own interests or wishes to help others or to contribute to the greater, common good.

In spiritual guidance, those who do not and cannot offer selflessness from the very beginning can never be truly devoted to this service, nor can they be successful, either. In such a noble task of mentoring people toward inner and outer harmony and prosperity, success comes when mentors are fully committed. Only those who are not hindered or enslaved by personal welfare, comfort, and desires—who can easily abandon worldly status and fame—can support and champion their cause and will ultimately reach success.

The Messenger of Allah ﷺ inculcated the spirit of self-sacrifice in everybody who supported his cause. He put this spirit into practice and was the best example to his close relations and others. Our mother Khadija, the Prophet's first wife, spent all her fortune for the cause she believed in, without even making Allah's Messenger ﷺ ask for her help. She spent her wealth for banquets to host Meccan disbelievers and teach them about Islam. When this glorious woman, who was one of the richest in Mecca before Islam, passed away, she had no means left behind to even buy a shroud for herself.

In addition to spending one's wealth, another form of sacrifice for devoted souls is *hijrah* (migration), i.e., to be able to leave his or her homeland when necessary for another place where they can have the freedom to practice their faith and speak their mind.

The Companions—whether rich or poor, young or old, male or female—and primarily Abu Bakr, Umar, Uthman, Ali, migrated from their hometown to another location. And while leaving their ancestral land, they had to leave all their property and possessions to the violent and cruel people of Mecca. They were able to take with them only a few provisions for their long journey.

The Emigrants (*Muhajirun*) from Mecca performed this self-sacrifice to represent and communicate the teachings they sincerely followed; and the Helpers (*Ansar*), who welcomed and embraced them in Medina, responded with another dimension of self-sacrifice. The Helpers, though poor farmers, welcomed their Meccan brothers—and later on sisters, too—with open arms and treated them with the utmost generosity.[113]

Spiritual mentors and guides of today must put into practice this understanding of self-sacrifice represented by the Companions of the Prophet, who are always considered to be the highest, most exemplary community of people. Today's mentors should at least sincerely try to give a similar performance as the Companions did. Otherwise, as we previously mentioned, they cannot be successful at conveying the message and mentoring people.

3.3. Prayer

Prayer is no less a quality of the spiritual mentor than the other qualities mentioned throughout the book. They expect their teaching to be effective only from Allah ﷻ, the Sole Owner of the heavens and the earth and all that is in and between them. Transformations of the heart take place only by His Divine Will and Omnipotence.

فَقَدْ كَذَّبْتُمْ فَسَوْفَ يَكُونُ لِزَامًا

"What has My Lord to do with you if you do not call on Him?" (al-Furqan 25:77).

This Divine decree is like a compass and makes the mentor turn towards Allah ﷻ through prayer.

The most eloquent and elegant words are sometimes ineffective on certain people. But the same people can change and may eventually be guided to truth and faith by wholehearted prayers done for them. For believers, prayer is like the most handy and multi-functional tool. For the mentor or guide, it is the first and the last, the ultimate refuge that we turn to all the time. Mentors first appeal to Allah's ﷻ help through prayer and then they start calling people to good. This is not an irrational action. On the contrary, appealing to Allah ﷻ first shows that the person is fully aware of the power of asking from Allah ﷻ and his or her personal initiatives in their proper places.

Here are a couple of examples that illustrate what a great elixir prayer is:

Allah's Messenger ﷺ tried every legitimate way to guide people but never gave up praying on their behalf. For example, he continuously supplicated to Allah ﷻ for Umar al-Khattab. Finally, one day, at an unexpected time, when there seemed to be no hope, Allah ﷻ bestowed the true faith on Umar. This was, we could say, a blessing bestowed in return for the prayers of Allah's Messenger ﷺ.[114]

One day, Abu Hurayrah came to the Messenger of Allah ﷺ and asked him to pray for his mother's guidance. Until that day, Abu Hurayrah could find no way to win his mother's heart. "*My Lord, give guidance to Abu Hurayrah's mother,*" said the Prophet ﷺ. Abu Hurayrah left the masjid with hope and ran home. As he was about to open the door, he heard his mother's voice from inside who said, "*Stay where you are, don't come in.*" While Abu Hurayrah was waiting outside, he heard she was washing herself. He thought his mother was probably having a bath. A little while later, his elderly mother opened the door, got out and recited the *shahadah*—there is no god but Allah ﷻ, and Muhammad is His Messenger ﷺ.

Abu Hurayrah was astonished to hear that his mother was reciting the *Shahadah* and announcing that she embraced Islam. Until that day he had worked so hard for her guidance, which, however, had to wait until the Prophet's prayer.[115]

3.4. Being rational and realistic

The spiritual mentor needs to be both rational and realistic. While evaluating events and conveying the message, he or she should take note of the interlocutor's level, and reason accordingly. To the extent they are reasonable and rational, the things they say and convey are welcomed correspondingly. Being rational does not mean to approach matters with cold logic, but to be sensible and act rationally according to the circumstances. Let me illustrate the issue with an outstanding example from Allah's Messenger ﷺ:

One day a young man showed up and asked the Prophet ﷺ to allow him to sleep with women. This shocked the Companions present. But the Prophet ﷺ calmly told the young man to come close and sit down. "*Would you like that for your mother?*" the Prophet ﷺ asked him. "*No, by Allah,*" the young man replied. "*Neither would anybody like that for their mothers. Would you like that for your daughter?*" asked the Prophet ﷺ. "*No, by Allah,*" the young man replied. "*Neither would anybody like that for their daughters. Would you like that for your sister?*" asked the Prophet. "*No, by Allah,*" replied the man. "*Neither would anybody like that for their sisters. Would you like that for your aunts?*" asked the Prophet. "*No, by Allah,*" said the young man. "*Neither would anybody like that for their aunts.*" Then, the Prophet ﷺ placed his hand on the young man and said, "*O Allah, forgive his sins, purify his heart, and guard his chastity.*" It is told that this young man led an upright life after this prayer.[116]

Julaibib is another young man whose story is worth mentioning here. Julaibib did not hold a respected status in society; he was not from a noble family, nor did he have any outstanding physical qualities. It was also told that he would mingle with women but did not know how to behave. To protect Julaibib from sin, the Prophet ﷺ asked for the hand of a girl from a well-known family. Although the parents were not so willing, the girl wished to comply with the Prophet's wish and gave her consent to marry Julaibib. Soon after, Julaibib was martyred in a battle. While everybody was looking for their friends or relatives on the battlefield, the Messenger of Allah, too, was looking for someone. "*Is there anyone missing amongst you?*" he asked those near him. Some said, "*No, Rasulullah. We are not missing anybody.*" The Prophet ﷺ then said, "*But I am missing Julaibib.*" They found him killed among seven people. He fought so heroically that he was able to kill seven before he got killed. Then, the Prophet ﷺ gave the good news that that would suffice to Julaibib's descendants until the Judgment Day: *"Julaibib is of me, and I am of Julaybib."*[117]

The Prophet ﷺ took into consideration human nature, offered a reasonable solution, and above all prayed for his friends' success, as a result of which people like Julaibib showed outstanding acts of courage.

3.5. Tolerance

The spiritual mentor ought to be understanding and tolerant. Tolerance never means to compromise one's faith or duty; it rather indicates broad-mindedness. A perfect example of tolerance is how the Prophet ﷺ treated the Meccan pagans when he conquered the city. They were the same pagans who did all they could to oppress Muslims and had left the Prophet ﷺ with no other choice but to leave the city. They had subjected all Muslims to the cruelest, most inhumane torments for many years.

On the day of the conquest, the Prophet ﷺ asked the Meccans what they were expecting him to do with them. "Goodness. You are a noble brother, son of a noble brother," the Meccans said. And they received nothing but goodness from the Prophet. "Go your way," said the Prophet, "for you are the freed ones."

لَا تَثْرِيبَ عَلَيْكُمُ الْيَوْمَ

"No reproach this day shall be on you" (Yusuf 12:92).

This verse reports what Prophet Yusuf said to his brothers. However, the subtlety here is that Allah's Messenger ﷺ showed this tolerance to those who were not his immediate family—showing, as it were, how his munificence was so grand, peace be upon them all.

3.6. Being caring

The spiritual mentor is one who cares and is concerned. He or she feels anguished and grieved by the deviation of people from the right path, by their breaking of Allah's ﷻ commandments, and by unethical and immoral acts. Stubborn defiance and denial of Allah ﷻ and heedlessness towards His call, values, and virtues make the mentor's heart bleed. In particular, moments when they are helpless in terms of mentoring and guidance, when their hands are tied up, they feel angst, a deep anxiety or dread about the human condition or the state of the world in general.

لَعَلَّكَ بَاخِعٌ نَفْسَكَ اَلَّا يَكُونُوا مُؤْمِن۪ينَ

"*You will torment yourself to death because they refuse to believe,*" (ash-Shu'ara 26:3) says the Qur'an, speaking about the Messenger of Allah's ﷺ state of mind, which was filled with angst and grief for those who did not take heed. Essentially, this state of mind exists—and should exist—in all mentors in accordance with the extent and seriousness of the disbelieving individuals' situation.

Muslim scholars and jurists over the ages have studied and expressed arguments on irreligiousness and denial and rejection of the sacred principles, religious teachings, and faith. However, in accordance with the system formulated by those scholars, and depending on the particular person and matter at hand, the person concerned needs to be educated and invited to faith by convincing arguments and proof explained down to the finest detail. A believer is not supposed to stay indifferent to the individuals who have psycho-spiritually suffered due to the rejection and denial of religion, for Islam's understanding of benevolence is against this. Every believer may feel grief and pain according to their own level of consciousness. However, the pain of the spiritual guide is deeper than that of everybody, since mentoring and guiding people to the individual and collective good, righteousness, and benevolence is the purpose of their existence.

We can remember at this point an example about Khalid ibn Walid, which we mentioned earlier. The Prophet ﷺ was very upset when he heard Khalid ibn Walid killed someone although that person said the words of testimony. The Prophet ﷺ supplicated, "*O Allah! I am free from what Khalid has done.*"[118]

This sensitivity of the Messenger of Allah ﷺ reflected on people around him. For example, Caliph Umar asked someone returning from the Yamama battle if anything serious had happened. The person said there was nothing serious but that someone from among them had renounced his faith. Umar stood up, his heart beating, and asked, "What have you done to him?" When the man answered, "We killed him," Umar sighed, just as Allah's Messenger ﷺ did, and then he raised his hands to his Lord: "*My Allah, I swear that I was not with them while they were doing this and I swear that I have not been pleased when I heard what they did.*"[119]

3.7. Spirituality

The mentor is a person of heart who has a strong connection with Allah ﷻ. The stronger their connection with Allah ﷻ, the more influence their words have on the mentee. As they draw closer to Allah ﷻ, He makes them even closer to Himself and thus becomes their sense of hearing with which they hear, and their sense of sight with which they see, and their hand with which they grip; He becomes the basis of all their actions.[22]

In other words, every action of the mentor starts to take place under the guidance and within the level of Allah's ﷻ approval. To the extent they act upon and practice what they know, Allah ﷻ teaches them what they do not know. Allah ﷻ always makes them discern and reach the truth. They can solve even the most complex issues quite easily. As they sincerely keep on acting this way, they stand out from all the rest, excel in society, and become the representative of the Straight Path, *al-sirat al-mustakim*.

22 Bukhari, riqaq 38: Allah's Messenger said, "… And the most beloved things with which My servant comes nearer to Me, is what I have enjoined upon him; and My servant keeps on coming closer to Me through performing *nawafil* [praying or doing extra deeds besides what is obligatory] till I love him, so I become his sense of hearing with which he hears, and his sense of sight with which he sees, and his hand with which he grips, and his leg with which he walks..."

Those who attain such a level begin to perpetually receive the most sacred blessings from Allah ﷻ. They become a center of appeal as a result of these blessings; and as they continue to guide others, thousands of people run to this heavenly shade around them. The wonderful appeal that has formed around the great spiritual mentors has always originated from their deep spiritual connection with Allah ﷻ.

The mentor who has acquired this state is considered to have reached the full certainty or conviction of faith (*yaqeen*). Reaching full certainty is to attain perfection in faith—i.e., belief in Allah without any doubt in the heart. Allah's Messenger ﷺ said, *"Certainty is all faith."*[120] Certainty is a state in which the human mind is convinced with evidence, improved by observation (*mushahada*), contemplation (*tafakkur*), ideas, and thoughts, and illuminated by inspiration. The carnal self is tamed with worship and prayers, and the heart made a polished mirror where Allah's ﷻ Names and Attributes are reflected as a result of self-control and introspection.[121]

Certainty is attaining *tawhid*, full conviction in Allah's ﷻ uniqueness. The person who attains certainty does not fear anybody, nor do they rely on expectations from other people. Such a person expects everything from Allah ﷻ alone, because he or she firmly believes that everything, good or bad, is willed and created by Allah ﷻ and comes into existence or takes places by His permission.

With such a conviction, all trials and tribulations, even the ultimate end—death—are not great concerns, or worries, let alone a deterrence. A person who has reached certainty acknowledges the reality of death and welcomes it smiling when it is due. In this way, he or she experiences the breezes and blessings of the Hereafter while they are still living in this world. They believe that they will see the heavenly realms and the most righteous of humanity they have been longing for when they will make that ultimate journey. For this reason, they are not gloomy and sad but content by what the Divine Will decrees about them. A hadith is reported to the effect as follows: *"Among my ummah, there are such brave people that, they stay smilingly among people [which is the expression of bespeaking Allah's favors]. They spend their nights in sighs and laments [which is the expression of their being mindful and fearing of Allah's punishment]. Their physical form is in this world; yet their heart is in the Heavens."*[122]

It must be a goal for every mentor or guide to be a person of certainty; they must take into consideration the world and Hereafter at the same time and thus attain the consciousness of Unity. These are the kinds of mentors we have expected and longed for. They are such mentors that they have no inclination at all towards the world for its worldly aspects. For them, the world is meaningful with the duty of mentoring and guiding. These teachers serve as if with the reviving breath of the Messiah, and the good character of Prophet Muhammad ﷺ, peace be upon them. And that's how every mentor should be, I think.

The late Tahir al-Mawlawi, who wrote a commentary on Mawlana's Rumi's *Mathnawi,* narrates: "*I was together with Atif Efendi of İskilip in the custodial prison. Atif Efendi was a learned man who was cognizant of the culture of his era. He had prepared a very serious written defense for the final trial in the court. The next day, he would appear in the court for his final hearing. In fact, the court had already made its decision, however we didn't know that at the time. Anyway, after the morning prayer, Atif Effendi tore the papers he wrote his defense on into pieces and threw it to the garbage can. I asked him 'What's the matter? Why have you torn it?' He replied: 'Last night, I saw the Messenger of Allah ﷺ in my dream. I was writing my defense. He said to me: 'Why is this eagerness of yours? Don't you want to come to us?' I answered: 'Sure I do, O Messenger of Allah!' This means it is time I met him, there is no need for defense!'*"

On the final day of the trial, Atif Efendi was sentenced to be executed, but he was at deep peace and greeted the death sentence with laughter. The decree was going to enable him to meet the most beloveds of Allah ﷻ, especially the Messenger of Allah ﷺ. Why should a person provided with such an opportunity not be happy? Why should a person following the path he believes to be true, who seeks Allah's approval in all aspects, who believes he is approaching Allah ﷻ and His Messenger ﷺ at every step, not be at peace? Such heroes can be killed, but they can never be defeated. In sum, the spiritual guide must always preserve this inner purity, sincerity, and uprightness that will ultimately lead him or her to success.

Those who devote themselves to Allah ﷻ and who try to gain only His approval will definitely attain all their wants and desires in the future, if not today. What does the one who finds Him lose? On the contrary, if one could not find Him, what worth would it be even if he owned the entire world?

What is essential is to meet the Lord with a pure and sound heart. Attaching so much importance to several trivialities can cause confusion and disorder. What we ask from Allah ﷻ is to preserve and maintain our hearts clean and pure until eternity, until the time we meet Him. We know that His mercy prevails over His wrath. What we desire is His approval, His pleasure, His Grace, and His Mercy ﷻ.

3.8. Enthusiasm

The spiritual mentor should carry out the duty of mentoring with love, enthusiasm, joyful zeal, and yearning. Conveying the truth and the message should be a mentor's true love and vocation. While this feeling is the most necessary one that should be hardwired into a mentor, it is not so easy to awaken and usually takes quite long to inculcate and realize it.

The Messenger of Allah ﷺ was able to implant this feeling in his community, making them lovers of the truth and conveying the message. Had he not done so, it would not have been possible for his *ummah* to realize this great duty by material means and causes only. They were so enthusiastic about it that they tried to observe it even in the most difficult circumstances. When the great Companion and commander Khalid ibn Walid confronted the Byzantine commander and his larger army, what he did first was to propose that he, the Byzantine commander, embrace faith.[123]

Such an attempt to guide even his enemy who he is about to fight can be explained with nothing but the ardor of conveying the truth. This love, yearning, and enthusiasm had a tremendous effect on almost all the Companions and is why they traveled and migrated to all corners of the world in order to convey the truth and message. The following is another example of this:

Khubayb was one of the early Muslims and Companion of the Messenger of Allah ﷺ. He was caught and kidnapped by the polytheists and taken to Mecca. They imprisoned him and forced him to renounce Islam. When their efforts were to no avail, they took him out into the main square to execute him. Khubayb was sad—but not because of the torture he was going through: he was sad because in that circumstance, he was unable to teach anybody about Islam. He was being taken to the gallows, his hands tied, and he unable to interact with anyone. He was continuously looking around and searching for someone to whom he could convey the truth. Among the delusional and noisy crowd, he could not see someone suitable for this. Although there were some Companions of the future among them, their hearts were not yet open to receiving the message at that time.

As his final request, he offered two *rak'ah*s of prayer and afterwards said, "*I would keep this last prayer of mine as long as I could, but I did not, lest you say, 'He fears death, that's why he prolongs the prayer.'*" Then he was made to mount the gallows. It was his last moments. Khubayb's eyes were still wandering around, but not looking for a person to save him from death. Even at the very last moment of his life, he was wondering if he could find someone and save *their* eternal life. For people like Khubayb, it was unfortunate not to find any person to teach even when they were about to give their last breath. At that instant, an unexpected opportunity arose for him.

One of the notables of the Meccan unbelievers asked him a question. The wording of the question was not important for Khubayb; he would take this opportunity to give them an answer full of wisdom and thus would have conveyed the truth in this last moment of his. Perhaps, his words could kindle a fire of faith in the hearts of who knows how many people in the future. The question was: "*Would you wish that [Prophet] Muhammad were in your place to be executed so that you could go free?*"

Such a question could not certainly be asked of a Muslim, especially someone like Khubayb. But he was trying to take the last opportunity he caught with this question. He bubbled over with excitement. He was filled with mixed feelings of happiness and sorrow. And he knew that the answer he would give to this question had to be as short as the last prayer he had just performed. He had to put his whole life into a single sentence. He had to speak in such a way that the entire history would remain speechless next to it, and it would be recorded as a great lesson in all times:

"*By Allah, I would not wish even a thorn to hurt his blessed foot in Medina in exchange for my being saved here!*"[124]

What a high example of loyalty and faithfulness to the truth! When Khubayb said this, the trouble he felt a few minutes before, for not having been able to perform the duty of guidance, likely came to an end. He probably felt a bit relieved. Just seconds before the spears penetrated his body, he sent a greeting of peace to Allah's Messenger ﷺ. He did not even bother to think whether his words of greeting would reach from Mecca to Medina. For, he knew the person he was greeting was Allah's exalted Prophet ﷺ and the One Who would convey it was the Almighty Creator ﷻ. His last, farewell words on the gallows were, "*Assalamu alaykum O Messenger of Allah.*" Allah's Messenger ﷺ was sitting in Medina with his Companions. It is told that he suddenly stood up and said "*Wa alaykum salam, O Khubayb.*"[125]

Every person who undertakes the blessed duty of mentoring and guidance ought to attain the same ardor and enthusiasm of Khubayb. If so, then they can interfere peacefully and constructively in this wrong course of history, put it on the right, true track, and deserve to be Allah's ﷻ "inheritors of the earth," as promised in all Divine Books.[126]

3.9. Purity of heart and spirit

The spiritual mentor must be in a state of the utmost purity of heart and spirit, especially while conveying the message to others. Their duty is pure, and so should their heart be. When they have a foggy spiritual state, this will cause interruptions in their relations with Allah ﷻ, and their words will have no influence on others. In their guidance, the spiritual mentor must aim for nothing but Allah's ﷻ approval and pleasure. As long as they do so, they will feel the support of Allah ﷻ, the spirit of His Messenger ﷺ, and the blessed, saintly people at their back. No one should have a doubt about it. Moreover, if one desires to receive Allah's ﷻ manifold blessings for their efforts, they must rely on the Divine power that will make it possible. Having recourse to other means brings nothing but loss.

Essentially, our understanding of Divine uniqueness (*tawhid*) requires this, too. Just as Allah ﷻ has no partner in His Divine Being, He has no partners in His creation and actions. He is the One Who will create the true guidance and misguidance. He is the One Who graces and disgraces whomever He wills. He makes one estimable or contemptible as He wills. It is He alone Who makes one succeed or fail as He wills.

It is true that striving to live a pure life is not easy, and life is full of trials and tribulations. However, the palace to be eventually reached beyond this impassable hill is truly blessed, too. Here are a few examples to illustrate the issue:

Abu Hanifa (d. 767), the scholar who is widely known as Al-Imam Al-A'zam—the great imam—was the eponymous founder of the Hanafi school of law. The Caliph of the time offered him the position of Chief Judge, one of the top official posts of the land. Abu Hanifa declined the offer because he knew that if he was to become the judge, he would never be able pass fair judgments. He aimed to preserve his inner purity and clarity of heart and soul. For this, he was punished by imprisonment and flogging. He suffered under the whip, but he still refused to accept the offer, which he considered a trap for his soul.[127]

Imam al-Shafi'i (d. 820) was another example. He was a prominent theologian, writer, and scholar and one of the first contributors to the principles of Islamic jurisprudence; like Abu Hanifa, he is one of the four great Sunni Imams. He showed every effort he could to shun proposals for official positions, too. He lived like a pariah among his kinsmen and refused all kinds of positions and statuses despite every pressure on him. Because of this, he had to spend the rest of his life in trouble. He kept a low profile and tried to keep his whereabouts as secret as possible. He changed places cautiously, so as not to be seen by anyone. To some extent, he tried not to be subjected to the difficulties that happened to Imam Abu Hanifa.[128]

Imam Ahmad ibn Hanbal was another example. He was one of the outstanding scholars of the Islamic sciences and the founder of one of the Sunni schools of law. The struggle he made for the sake of the Qur'an will never be forgotten by history. He remained steadfast throughout his whole life in his view that the Qur'an is the word of Allah ﷻ and was not created.[129] The oppressive regime of the time wanted to impose a contrary view, and those Islamic scholars who did not accept it were punished and imprisoned. If he had talked diplomatically and used allusive words, he would have easily managed to go free, but he had not deigned to use any of these. He narrated a memory of his as follows:

"I was screaming in pain when I was being whipped the first few days. Then, a criminal was brought to prison. He said to me: 'O imam! Are

you screaming while you are here for a cause you believe to be true? I am here because of a crime, and they are whipping me as much as they do to you, yet I am still not screaming.' After that, whenever they started to whip me, the words of that criminal used to come to my mind. Then I was trying to endure it. I clenched my teeth and tried not to raise my voice or say anything even at times I was subjected to most violent blows of the whip."

This great imam spent many days and months in this painful ordeal. He showed his willpower even at times when he was the most powerless. He displayed a legendary heroism without compromising a word of what he had said on the first day. Imam al-Shafi'i, who led low profile life in those days, saw our Prophet ﷺ in his dream. Allah's Messenger ﷺ said to Imam al-Shafi'i: "*Convey my greetings to Ahmad ibn Hanbal. Tell him to bear it for some more time [let him grit his teeth a little more]. He will soon come to me.*"

Imam al-Shafi'i immediately sent one of his men to the prison because it was impossible for him to go there. He also sent a shirt and said, "*Tell the imam to wear this shirt and let it touch his blessed skin.*" The man visited Ahmad ibn Hanbal and told him everything. Ahmad ibn Hanbal heard that Allah's Messenger ﷺ sent him greetings and forgot about everything he had suffered and started to shed tears of happiness.

When his man came back with the shirt, Imam al-Shafi'i rubbed it on his face and said: "*I hope the fire of hell will not touch the face which is rubbed with the shirt Ahmad ibn Hanbal's skin touched.*"[130]

Conclusion

Here is a summary of the points—deduced from Islamic teachings—mentioned throughout the book concerning the main principles to be adopted by spiritual guides and mentors:

1. Conveying the message, calling to good, preventing wrong, and spiritual mentoring and guidance, are the most sacred of all duties. This is so because Allah ﷻ sent the Prophets, His most distinguished servants, to perform this duty.

2. Spiritual mentoring is normally a *fard al-kifaya*,[23] (i.e., a responsibility on the whole community, not specifically on individuals). Yet, it has become a very important duty, a supra-obligation, since it is among the matters most neglected in our day and age. Neglecting mentoring and guidance is definitely not excusable and permissible.

3. It must be feared that a person who died in negligence of this duty might have died in hypocrisy. For, he or she has abandoned the duty of calling to good, which is more important, meritorious, and rewarding than their own personal obligations.

4. We hope for a society in which the duty of spiritual mentoring is performed that they are under Allah's ﷻ mercy and protection from earthly and heavenly disasters. Even if a few people in a community can do this sacred duty, the whole community is under Allah's ﷻ protection. If the opposite is the case, the result will be the opposite, too. In other words, such a community in which this sacred duty is abandoned can be pun-

23 *fard al-kifaya* is a communal obligation, a social responsibility that must be discharged by the Muslim community as a whole. If enough members of the Muslim community discharge the obligation, the remaining Muslims are freed from the responsibility before Allah. However, if a communal obligation is not sufficiently discharged, then every individual Muslim must act to address the deficiency. "Commanding good and forbidding evil" comes under this communal obligation, social responsibility, and civic service.

ished—or maybe even destroyed. The mass destructions that took place in past nations are the most obvious examples of this.

5. This sacred duty must be observed at all possible social levels: individual, national, and international. A true Muslim is an essential agent of peace and order in society. Where such true Muslims do not exist or have no influence, chaos, disorder, and anarchy may prevail. The true Muslim is a barrier or bulwark against disorder, violence, and terror—and this heavily depends on whether the Muslim performs their duty to mentor and guide properly and with efficacy or not.

6. وَالْمُؤْمِنُونَ وَالْمُؤْمِنَاتُ بَعْضُهُمْ اَوْلِيَاءُ بَعْضٍ يَأْمُرُونَ بِالْمَعْرُوفِ وَيَنْهَوْنَ عَنِ الْمُنْكَرِ وَيُقِيمُونَ الصَّلٰوةَ وَيُؤْتُونَ الزَّكٰوةَ وَيُطِيعُونَ اللّٰهَ وَرَسُولَهُ اُولٰٓئِكَ سَيَرْحَمُهُمُ اللّٰهُ اِنَّ اللّٰهَ عَزِيزٌ حَكِيمٌ

The believers, both men and women: they are guardians, confidants, and helpers of one another. They enjoin and promote what is right and good, and forbid and try to prevent the evil, and they establish the Prescribed Prayer in conformity with its conditions, and pay the Prescribed Purifying Alms. They obey Allah and His Messenger. They are the ones whom Allah will treat with mercy. Surely Allah is All-Glorious with irresistible might, All-Wise. (at-Tawbah 9:71)

The duty of "calling to good and preventing wrong" is a distinguishing characteristic or sign of the believer. It should not be considered separately from one's faith. For, when the Qur'an says in the verse above that believers are helpers of one another, it points to the main principle that sustains this protection and reminds us that it is the most sacred duty. As for the hypocrites, they are all alike (at-Tawbah 9:67). They have an understanding of their own, private interests, but they are not protectors of one another. They therefore prevent the good and encourage individuals to do wrong.

7. It is Allah ﷻ Who will protect His religion. However, this protection depends on the efforts and patronage of all believers—men and women—and on the condition that at least a certain group of individuals uphold this faith by fulfilling the duty of conveying the message.

8. Knowledge of faith, practicing it in one's own life, and teaching it to

others by spiritual guidance are three aspects of one reality. They cannot be separated from one another. Knowledge is essential in mentoring and guidance; and sincerely practicing what one says is the soul of mentoring and guidance.

9. The spiritual mentor must know very well the Islamic truths and be aware of the realities of the era they live in. Those who do not know anything about their time are basically living in a dark tunnel, isolated from realities. Their attempts to invite people into this dark tunnel and teach them something there is a miserable effort.

10. A spiritual mentor must attune his or her heart to the Qur'an. It is very difficult and even impossible for a person who cannot do this to speak in the name of Islam and to convey the Islamic truths.

11. Spiritual mentors should be very careful to make sure all the means they use for conveying the message are legitimate. A legitimate goal can only be achieved by legitimate means. This is the way Allah's Messenger ﷺ and His noble Companions followed. What we need is not militants, who consider every method to be legitimate in order to reach their ambition; we need spiritual mentors with the spirit of the Companions, paying the utmost attention to using legitimate means. These are the only ones who will uphold the truth and beauty of the religion and convey it those who need it all over the world.

12. Spiritual mentors must absolutely live and practice what they teach. The opposite behavior is a sign of hypocrisy, and the believer must strictly avoid such a situation. There can be no positive effect and blessings in the words of those who do not act upon and practice what they say. They flare suddenly but extinguish quickly. They are of no use at bringing people to the truth.

13. Spiritual mentors must always preserve their modesty and humility, which are attributes of noble character. Faith is the very nobility itself. The mentor must act nobly (as is expected of every true believer). This is the character of Allah's Messenger ﷺ, which every spiritual guide must take on.

14. Spiritual mentors must not intermingle with political authorities, state officials, and elitists in a way that can be abused for their interests,

except for the necessity of conveying the message and mentoring. Utmost care and meticulousness in this regard are the most essential conditions for the mentor to preserve their status and dignity.

15. Spiritual mentors must be very consistent, persistent, and insistent, at the duty of mentoring and guidance. This consistence, perseverance, and insistence is the evidence of their respect towards their duty and what they teach. The mentor has to hold in high regard and honor the matters Allah ﷻ holds in high regard. Otherwise, they will have denied the things they said.

16. Spiritual mentors must not conflict with and oppose the laws of innate, inherent human nature. They should always show insight and prudence in their spiritual guidance. It is definitely wrong to ignore or deny some weaknesses and desires that exist in humans. What is essential is to be able to channel them towards the good, the best, and the most approved direction.

17. Trials and tribulations are the inevitable company and the fate of this duty. Spiritual mentors have to acknowledge from the very outset the likelihood of hardship and suffering along the way.

18. Spiritual mentors are heroes of compassion. They must never, ever try to force people to accept the truth by means of coercion.

19. One of the most important aspects of the spiritual guide is altruism and self-sacrifice. Every spiritual guide should take Allah's ﷻ apostles and the disciples of Prophets as exemplars of magnanimity of heart and a sense of self-sacrifice. Those who do not have this quality can hardly be a notable spiritual mentor. Such a duty requires self-devotion and altruism.

20. Spiritual mentors are people of prayer. Prayer is the essence of sincerity and purity of intention.

21. Spiritual mentors are people of common sense, reason, and reality. The success of their message depends on the extent of their sensibility and rationality.

22. Spiritual mentors are very sensitive about the faith and spiritual

well-being of other people. Events of disbelief and its ensuing problems grieve them deeply and make their heart bleed on other people's behalf.

23. Spiritual guides always love their duty and do it with enthusiasm. In fact, it is impossible for them to succeed unless they are enamored of and dedicated to the task of mentoring and guidance.

24. Inner depth and spiritual profundity are necessary qualities of the spiritual mentor. Spiritual depth signifies, as it were, that he or she has attained certainty of knowledge and faith. And those who attain certainty are also endowed with all virtues.

25. Spiritual mentors, while conveying the message and guiding, must have the clarity and purity of their heart and spirit. And in order to have Allah's ❁ and His Messenger's ❁ approval and support behind them, they have to live a life as pure as their message and duty. Such a life can only be realized with the purity of one's heart.

Notes

1 Bukhari, Bad'ul-halq 7; Muslim, Jihad 111.

2 Bediüzzaman Said Nursi, *Tarihçe-i Hayat*, p. 616.

3 Ebû Ya'lâ, al-Musnad 11/304; at-Tabarani, al-Mu'jamu'l awsat 9/129

4 ad-Daylami, al-Musnad 3/586; al-Maqdisi, Zahiratu'l-huffadh 4/2227.

5 Ahmad ibn Hanbal, al-Musnad 6/68, 431, 432; at-Tabarani, al-Mu'jamu'l Kabir 24/257.

6 Ahmad ibn Hanbal, al-Musnad 4/199; Ibn Abdilbarr, al-Istiab 3/1190; Ibn Asakir, Tarihu Dimashk 46/193.

7 Hud 11:42-43.

8 al-An'am 6:74.

9 Bukhari, Tafsiru surah (9) 16, (28) 1, aymân 19; Muslim, iman 41.

10 Ibn Asâkir, Tarihi Dimashk 49/152; Ibn Adiyy, al-Kamil 6/111.

11 Bediüzzaman Said Nursi, *Tarihçe-i Hayat* p. 616.

12 Bukhari, Tafsiru surah (2) 1, tawhid 36; Muslim, iman 322, 326, 327.

13 Bukhari, Fadail ashab 9; Muslim, Fadail as-sahabah 32-35.

14 al-Hakim, al-Mustadrak 3/270; Ibn Abdilbarr, al-Istiab 3/1084.

15 Bukhari, manakıbu'l-ansar 3, niqah 7, buyu' 1; Tirmidhi, birr 22.

16 Bukhari, Fadail ashâb 9; Muslim, Fadail as-sahabah 32-35.

17 Bukhari, Fadail ashab 9; Muslim, Fadail as-sahabah 32-35.

18 Muslim, iman 78; Tirmidhi, fitan 11; Abu Dawud, salat 239.

19 Muslim, Jihad 58; Ahmad ibn Hanbal, al-Musnad 1/30-32.

20 Tirmidhi, Manaqib 25; Abu Dawud, sünnet 8; Ibn Majah, mukaddimah 11.

21 Bukhari, adhan 95; Muslim, salat 158.

22 Bukhari, Ilm, 45; Jihad, 15; Muslim, Imarat, 149-151.

23 Ibn Sa'd, at-Tabaqatu'l-kubra 1/207; at-Tabara, Tarihu'l-umam wa'l-muluk 2/132; Ibn Hibban, as-Sikat 2/9.

24 Abu Dawud, janaiz, 56; Ahmad ibn Hanbal, al-Musnad 1/461.

25 Ahmad ibn Hanbal, al-Musnad 1/202, 461, 4/252, 5/290-291; at-Tayalisi, al-Musnad p. 46.

26 Bukhari, iman 42, mawaqit 3, zakât 2, shurut 1; Muslim, iman 97.

27 ad-Daylami, al-Musnad 2/174.

28 Bukhari, iman 42; Muslim, iman 95; Tirmidhi, birr 17.

29 Muslim, imarat 133; Tirmidhi, ilim 14; Abu Dawud, adab 114-115.

30 Muslim, zakat 69; Tirmidhi, ilm 15; Ibn Majah, mukaddimah 14.

31 Bukhari, iman 4, 5; Muslim, iman 64-65.

32 Bukhari, adab 27; Muslim, birr 66.

33 Tirmidhi, tafsir'ul sura (5) 6; Abu Dawud, melâhim 17; Ibn Majah, fiten 20.

34 Tirmidhi, tafsir'ul sura (5) 17, fitan 8; Abu Dawud, malahim 17.

35 This is a weak hadith. Ahmad ibn Hanbal, al-Musnad 5/390; Ibn Abi Shayba, al-Musannaf 7/460, 530.

36 Tirmidhi, fiten 9; Ahmad ibn Hanbal, al-Musnad 5/188.

37 Tirmidhi, zühd 39; Ahmad ibn Hanbal, al-Musnad 6/18.

38 Ibn Kathir, al-Bidayah wa'n-nihaya 3/95.

39 See Bukhari, tafsir'ul surah (11) 5; Muslim, birr 61.

40 Bukhari, sharika 6, shahadah 30; Tirmidhi, fitan 12.

41 at-Tabarani, al-Mu'jamu'l-kabir 20/363; Ibn Hisham, as-Siratu'n-nabawiyyah 2/281-284; Ibn Sa'd, at-Tabakatu'l-kubra 1/220.

42 Ibn Hisham, as-Siratu'n-nabawiyyah 2/284; Ibn Asakir, Tarihu'l Dimashk 9/83-84

43 Ibn Sa'd, at-Tabaqatu'l-kubra 2/41, 3/121.

44 Ibn Sa'd, at-Tabaqatu'l-kubra 3/121; Ibnu'l-Mubarak, al-Jihad s.82; Ibnu'l-Esir, Usdu'l-ghaba 5/193.

45 Halid M. Halid, Rijalun hawla'r-Rasul, p. 52

46 al-Munawi, Fayzu'l-kadir 1/225, 4/399, 5/50; al-Ajluni, Kashfu'l-hafa 2/343.

47 al-Jumu'ah 62:5.

48 Tirmidhi, ilm 19; Abu Dawud, ilm 1; Ibn Majah, mukaddimah 17.

49 Anbiya, 21:105.

50 Tirmidhi, ilim 19; Dârimî, mukaddime 29, 32.

51 Tirmidhi, ilim 3; Abu Dawud, ilim 9; Ibn Majah, mukaddimah 24.

52 Bediüzzaman Said Nursi, *The Letters*, "The Second Letter." NJ: The Light, 2014, pp.13-14.

53 Al-Ghazzali, *Ihya Ulumiddin Vol.1,* p. 57.

54 Al-Ghazzali, *Ihya Ulumiddin Vol.2*, p. 353.

55 Bukhari, jihad 131, maghazi 38, daawat 50, 67; Muslim, dhikr 44-45.

56 Bukhari, ahqam 13; Muslim, salat 182.

57 Ahmad ibn Hanbal, al-Musnad 3/492, 4/63, 4/341, 5/371, 376.

58 See at-Tabarani, al-Mu'jamu'l-kabir 4/27; Ibn Hajar, al-Isaba 2/87

59 See Tirmidhi, daawat 69; Ahmad ibn Hanbal, al-Musnad 4/444

60 Tirmidhi, qiyamah 42; Ibn Majah, iqamah 174; Darimi, salat 156.

61 Bediüzzaman Said Nursi, The Fourteenth Ray.

62 al-Kalabazi, a*t-Taarruf* 1/5; al-Gazali, *Ihya ulumi'd-din* 4/306; al-Jurjani, a*t-Ta'rifat* 1/564.

63 Ibnu'l-Jawzi, Sifatu's-safwah 1/736; Ibnu'l-Asir, Usdu'l-ghaba 4/540; Ibn Hajar, al-Isaba 1/98, 5/675.

64 See Ibn Abdilbarr, al-Istiab 4/1829; Ibnu'l-Asir, Usdu'l-ghaba 7/101.

65 al-Kafi, Vol. 1, p. 23. See ad-Daylami, al-Musnad 1/398; Ibn Hajar, Lisanu'l-mizan 6/274; al-Ajluni, Kashfu'l-hafa 1/226, 2/251.

66 Ahmad ibn Hanbal, az-Zuhd 1/54; Abu Nuaym, Hilyetu'l-awliya 2/382. Ahmad ibn Hanbal, az-Zuhd 1/54; Abu Nuaym, Hilyetu'l-awliya 2/382.

67 Ahmad ibn Hanbal, al-Musnad 1/22, 44; Ibn Hibban, as-Sahih 1/281.

68 Ibn Hibban, as-Sahih 2/386.

69 Muslim, salatu'l-musafirin 118; Tirmidhi, salat 158.

70 Bukhari, tahajjud 9; Muslim, salatu'l-musafirin 204.

71 *Al-mala' al-a'la*: the supreme assembly of angels.

72 Bukhari, adhan 51; Muslim, salat 90.

73 Ahmad ibn Hanbal, al-Musnad 2/381; Ibn Sa'd, at-Tabakatu'l-kubra 2/66; al-Vakidi, Kitabu'l-maghazi 2/445-447.

74 Bukhari, hiba 1; Muslim, zuhd 28.

75 Bukhari, riqaq 17; Ahmad ibn Hanbal, al-Musnad 6/73.

76 Bukhari, zakat 60, jihad 188; Muslim, zakat 161.

77 Ahmad ibn Hanbal, *Musnad*, 6720.

78 See at-Tabari, Jamiu'l-bayan 28/127; Ibn Abi Hatim, at-Tafsir 3/722, 10/3358; Ibn Kathir, Tafsiru'l-Qur'an 4/378.

79 at-Tabarani, al-Mu'jamu'l awsat 8/130; Ibn Sa'd, at-Tabaqatu'l-kubra 3/350-351.

80 Abu Dawud, sunnah 25.

81 See Surah Nasr, 110: 1-3.

82 See Ibn Sa'd, at-Tabaqatu'l-kubra 3/293; Ibn Asakir, Tarihu Dimashk 44/315.

83 Ahmed b. Hanbal, al-Musnad 1/72; Ibnu'l-Asir, Usdu'l-ghaba 3/594.

84 Ahmad ibn Hanbal, al-Musnad 3/120, 180, 231, 239; at-Tabarani, al-Mu'jamu'l awsat 8/144.

85 at-Tabarani, al-Mu'jamu'l-kabir 20/138; al-Mu'jamu'l awsat 6/342.

86 See Ibn Hisham, as-Siratu'n-nabawiyya 5/63; Abu Ya'la, al-Musnad 6/120.

87 Bukhari, Siqayatu'l-Hajj, 25. Hadith no 1635.

88 See Bukhari, mazalim 25, niqah 83, riqaq 17; Muslim, libas 37.

89 See Sibli Numani, *Hz. Omer ve Devlet Idaresi (Umar and Ruling a Country)*, 2/393-394.

90 Abu Nuaym, Hilyatu'l-awliya 8/80, 81.

91 Abu Nuaym, Hilyetü'l-awliya 8/81.

92 See Sunan Ibn Majah, hadith no 255, 256. Abu Mansur al-Daylami, Firdaws, 1:155, 3:75.

93 See Muslim, *fadailu's-sahaba* 45: Ibn Majah, *zuhd* 7; Abdurrazzak, *Tafsiru's San'ani* 2/207-208; at-Tabari, *Jamiu'l-bayan* 7/200-205.

94 Narrated by Abu Ya'alaa in his Musnad: 6/10. See also Ahmad ibn Hanbal, *al-Musnad* 5/236; at-Tabarani, *al-Mu'jamu'l-kabir* 5/197.

95 Bukhari, maghazi 58, ahqam 3; Nasai, adabu'l-kudat 17.

96 See Ahmad ibn Hanbal, al-Musnad 1/159; at-Tabari, Jamiu'l-bayan 19/122; al-Bayhaqi, Dalailu'n-nubuwwah 2/179-180.

97 at-Tabarani, al-Mu'jamu'l-kabir 3/268, 22/438; Ibn Asakir, Tarihu Dimashk 11/407, 52/306, 57/182.

98 Sahih al-Bukhari volume 5, Book 57, Hadith 27; Sahih al-Bukhari Vol. 6, Book 60, Hadith 339; Sahih al-Bukhari volume 5, Book 58, Hadith 195,

99 Ibn Asakir, Tarihu Dimashk 30/47, 50, 52; Ibn Kathir, al-Bidaya wa'n-nihaya 3/29-30.

100 See Ibn Hisham, as-Siratu'n-nabawiyya 2/162; Ibn Sa'd, at-Tabaqatu'l-kubra 3/246-248, 4/136; at-Tabarani, *al-Mu'jamu'l-kabir* 24/303.

101 See Ibn Hisham, as-Siratu'n-nabawiyya 2/159; Abu Nuaym, Hilyatu'l-awliya 1/148.

102 Bukhari, at-Tarihu'l-kabir 7/421. See also at-Tabarani, *al-Mu'jamu'l-kabir* 1/85.

103 at-Tabarani, *al-Mu'jamu'l-kabir* 1/122; al-Hakim, al-Mustadrak 3/406.

104 Ibn Asakir, Tarihu Dimashk 27/359; Ibnu'l-Asir, Usdu'l-ghaba 3/214; *Mujahid, Abdul Malik (2012). Golden Stories of Umar Ibn Al-Khattab.*

105 Abu Nuaym, Hilyatu'l-awliya 7/109, 8/42; Hatib al-Baghdadi, Tarihu Baghdad 3/155.

106 Sunan al-Tirmidhi 2360

107 Bukhari, bad'u'l-halq 6, maghazi 30, adab 91; Muslim, Fadail as-sahaba 153.

108 Abu Dawud, taharat 4; Nasaî, taharat 36; Ibn Majah, taharat 16.

109 See as-Suyuti, al-Hasaisu'l-kubrâ 1/80, 85, 91.

110 Bukhari, anbiya 40, riqaq 26; Muslim, fadail 17-19.

111 Bukhari, bad'u'l-halq 7; Muslim, jihad 111.

112 Bukhari, anbiya 54; Muslim, jihad 104-105.

113 Bukhari, manaqibu'l-ansar 3, niqah 7, buyu' 1; Tirmidhi, birr 22.

114 Ibn Kathir, al-Bidayah wa'n-nihaya 3/31; Ibnu'l-Asir, Usdu'l-ghaba 4/148; Ibn Sa'd, at-Tabaqatu'l-kubra 3/268.

115 Muslim, Fadail as-sahaba 158; Ahmad ibn Hanbal, al-Musnad 2/319.

116 Ahmad ibn Hanbal, al-Musnad (22211) 5/256; at-Tabarani, *al-Mu'jamu'l-kabir* 8/162, 183.

117 Muslim, Fadail as-sahaba 131; Ahmad ibn Hanbal, al-Musnad 4/420, 421, 425.

118 Bukhari, maghazi 58, ahqam 3; Nasai, adabu'l-qudat 17.

119 Muwatta, akdiya 58; ash-Shafii, al-Musnad 1/321; Saad Ibn Mansur, as-Sunan 2/266.

120 at-Tabarani, *al-Mu'jamu'l-kabir* 9/104; Abu Nuaym, Hilyatu'l-awliya 5/34; al-Bayhaqi, Shuabu'l-iman 1/74.

121 For more on "Certainty," see Fethullah Gülen, *Key Concepts in the Practice of Sufism-1,* 'Yaqin (Certainty)', Tughra Books: NJ. 2011. pp. 125-129. Also at https://fgulen.com/en/fethullah-gulens-works/key-concepts-in-the-practice-of-sufism-1/yaqin-certainty.

122 al-Hakim, al-Mustadrak 3/19; al-Bayhaqi, Shuabu'l-iman 1/478.

123 Ibn Asakir, Tarihu Dimashk 2/160; Ibn Kathir, al-Bidayah wa'n-nihaya 7/13.

124 Bukhari, maghazi 10; Ahmad ibn Hanbal, al-Musnad 2/294; at-Tayalisi, al-Musnad p. 338; at-Tabarani, *al-Mu'jamu'l-kabir* 5/259-261; Ibn Hisham, as-Siratu'n-nabawiyya 4/126; Ibn Sa'd, at-Tabakatu'l-kubra 3/68.

125 See Ibn Kathir, al-Bidayah wa'n-nihaya 4/66; Ibn Hajar, Fathu'l-bari 7/384.

126 al-Anbiya 21:105.

127 Zahabi, Tazkiratu'l-huffadh 1/168-169; Ibn Hallikan, Wafayatu'l-a'yan 5/407; Hatip al-Baghdadi, Tarihu Baghdad 13/326-328.

128 Abu Nuaym, Hilyatu'l-awliya 9/112.

129 See Abu Nuaym, Hilyetu'l-awliya, 9/206, az-Zahabi, Siyaru a'lami'n-nubala 11/239-240.

130 Ibn Asakir, Tarihu Dimashk 5/311-312.

Index

A

Abbasids 70
Abdullah ibn Hudhafah as-Sahmi 144
Abdullah ibn Mas'ud 125
Abdullah ibn Salaam 99, 100
Abraham. *See* Ibrahim, the Prophet
Abu Bakr 30, 59, 60, 70, 129, 143, 154
Abu Hanifa 94, 111, 165
Abu Hurayrah 145
Abu Jahl 44, 140
Abu Ya'la 19, 175
Abyssinia 28, 46, 47
Adam 13, 14, 16, 17, 24, 80, 92
Age of Happiness 11, 27, 38, 128
ahl al-Sunnah 25
Ahmad ibn Hanbal 60, 111, 165, 166, 173-176
Aisha 16, 124-126, 128
Al-Farabi 111
Ali ibn Abu Talib 134, 146
Al-Imam Al-A'zam. *See* Abu Hanifa
al-insan al-kamil 84
Al-Layth ibn Sa'd 94
al-mala' al-a'la 125
almsgiving 41
Ammar ibn Yasir 137, 143
Amr ibn al-As 27, 28, 47
Andalusia 69
Ansar 154
Antioch 92
Ashamah. *See* Negus
Atif Efendi of İskilip 161
awliya 55, 56, 174-177
Ayka, people of al- 24

B

Babylon 58
Badr, the Battle of 74
al-Baqi' 133
Bediüzzaman 17, 21, 30, 40, 93, 105, 173, 174. *See also* Nursi
Bilal al-Habashi 137, 144

C

carnal soul 21
ceremonialism 115, 116
Children of Israel 58, 99, 117
Christianity 144
Companions of the Prophet 20, 21, 32, 36, 44, 47, 128, 154
Cyrus 58

D

Day of Judgment 26, 30, 54, 73, 94, 145
Dead Sea 69
disbelief 21, 27, 28, 41, 42, 70, 71, 89, 102, 103, 152, 153, 171
Divine ethics 112
Divine Will and Decree 60
Durrah bint Abu Lahab 25

E

Egypt 16, 58, 70, 143
Ethiopia 46

F

Fakhr al-din ar-Razi 111
family 26, 31, 33, 36, 43, 68, 77, 108, 109, 118, 124, 129, 145,

151, 157, 158
fard al-kifaya 167
five essentials (necessities) 18
formalism 52, 115, 116
Fudayl ibn 'Iyad 94

G

Ghazali, Imam al- 87, 104, 111

H

Habib al-Najjar 92
Hansa, the poet 111
Harith ibn Harith 143
Harun al-Rashid 95
Hasan (the Prophet's grandson) 126
Hasan al-Basri 25
Hassan ibn Thabit 146
Hatim al-Asam 133, 134
Hell 9, 30, 55, 57, 61, 115, 129
hijrah 154
Hud, the Prophet 15, 16, 23, 68, 69, 123, 173
Hudhayfah ibn Al-Yaman 60
hypocrites 56, 57, 116, 119, 120, 131, 168

I

Ibn Abbas 145
Ibn Abi'd-Dunya 19
Ibn Mas`ud 137
Ibn Muqatil 133, 134
Ibn Rushd 111
Ibn Sina 111
Ibrahim, the Prophet 15, 29, 67, 80, 94, 143
Ibrahim ibn Adham 94
intercession 30
Isa, the Prophet 16, 48, 92, 116, 143
Islamic world 59
Israiliyyat 24

J

Jacob. *See* Yaqub, the Prophet
Ja'far ibn Abu Talib 48
jamalullah 96
Jarir ibn Abdullah al-Bajali 49
Jesus. *See* Isa, the Prophet
Jethro. *See* Shu'aib, the Prophet
Jibril 130
John. *See* Yahya, the Prophet
Joseph. *See* Yusuf, the Prophet
Judeans 58
Julaibib 156, 157

K

Ka'ba 24, 62, 66, 111, 143
kalima tawheed 139
Khabbab ibn al Aratt 137
Khalid ibn Walid 139, 146, 162
Khaybar 32, 33
Khubayb ibn Adiy 162-164
kuntum 34

L

Labid, the poet 111
Luqman 50, 145
Lut, the Prophet 24, 67, 68, 69

M

mahabbah 82
majnun 64
Malik, Imam 111
ma'rifah 82
marriage 43
ma'ruf 10, 11, 72, 77
Mary. *See* Maryam
Maryam 48, 116
maskh 67
Mathnawi 161
Mawlana Halid al-Baghdadi 104
Mecca 46-48, 74, 81, 132, 138, 140, 143, 154, 162, 164

Medina 74, 81, 133, 154, 163, 164
Moses. *See* Musa, the Prophet
Mount Sinai 80, 109
Muadh ibn Jabal 146
Muhajirun 154
Muhammad ibn Muqatil 133
mujahid 54
munkar 11, 35
muruwwah 72
Musa, the Prophet 16, 59, 80, 96, 109, 143
Mus'ab ibn Umayr 74, 146
mushahada 160
mutrafin 62
muttaqi 88

N

nasihah 51
Nebuchadnezzar 58
Negus 46-49
Noah. *See* Nuh, the Prophet
Nuh, the Prophet 14-16, 29, 63, 64, 65, 71, 80, 143
Nursi, Said 17, 30, 40, 89, 93, 105, 173, 174. *See also* Bediüzzaman

O

obligatory charity 49
Ottomans 70, 131

P

Paradise 9, 30, 38, 61, 73, 82, 87, 96, 105, 133, 142, 152
pilgrimage 41, 95
Pompeii 69
prescribed prayers 41
privation 144, 145
Prophethood 13, 64, 140, 146
Purifying Alms 55, 168

Q

Qur'anic ethics 10

R

Rabbani, Imam 87, 104
Raja' ibn Haywah 136
Rawda 133
Rightly Guided Caliphs 11, 136
Romans 70, 144
Rumi 87, 161

S

Sa'ad al-Din al-Taftazani 102
Sabean 143
Sa'd ibn Abi Waqqas 38
Sa'd ibn Ubada 74
Sahaba 25
Salahuddin Al Ayyubi 75, 76
Salih, the Prophet 65, 66, 67
Sassanids 70, 129
Satan 21
Seljuks 70
Shafi'i, Imam al- 111, 165, 166
shahadah 156, 174
Shu'aib, the Prophet 24, 123
Sodom and Gomorrah 24, 67, 69
Straight Path 93, 117, 159
Sufyan al-Thawri 94, 95
Suhayb al-Rumi 137

T

Tabiun 25
tabligh 11
tafakkur 160
tahajjud 102, 125, 129, 175
Tahir al-Mawlawi 161
Taif 152
Talha ibn Ubaydullah 144
Tanafisi, Imam al- 134
tawhid 160, 164, 173
Thamud, people of 65, 66

Torah 100
Turkey 27

U

Ubaydullah ibn Abdullah 136
ulu'l azm 14
Umar ibn al-Khattab 32, 38, 128, 129, 133, 144, 154, 155, 159, 175, 176
Umar ibn Abd al-Aziz 136, 137
Umayyads 70, 136
ummah 21, 30, 50, 59, 73, 119, 124, 126, 129, 131, 150, 160, 162
Uqba ibn Abi Mu'ait 143
Usayd ibn Hudayr 74
Uthman ibn Affan 129, 154

Y

Yahya, the Prophet 16, 143
yaqeen 160
Yaqub, the Prophet 150
Yunus Emre 80, 141
Yusuf, the Prophet 150, 157

Z

Zainab, the Prophet's daughter 143
zakat 49
zamzam 66
Zayd ibn Haritha 152
Zechariah, the Prophet 16
Zubayr ibn al-Awwam 144